The ~~~~ of
CAIRO
and LUXOR

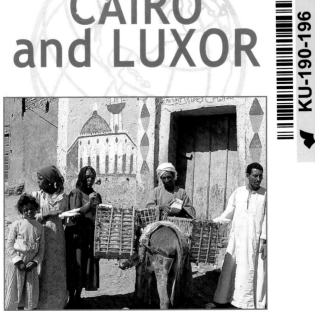

ROBIN GAULDIE

NEW
HOLLAND

GLOBETROTTER™

Second edition published in 2007
by New Holland Publishers (UK) Ltd
London • Cape Town • Sydney • Auckland
10 9 8 7 6 5 4 3 2

website: www.newhollandpublishers.com

Garfield House, 86 Edgware Road
London W2 2EA
United Kingdom

80 McKenzie Street
Cape Town 8001
South Africa

Unit 1, 66 Gibbes Street,
Chatswood, NSW 2067
Australia.

218 Lake Road
Northcote, Auckland
New Zealand

Distributed in the USA by
The Globe Pequot Press, Connecticut

ISBN 978 1 84537 835 6

Publishing Manager: Thea Grobbelaar
DTP Cartographic Manager: Genené Hart
Editors: Carla Zietsman, Thea Grobbelaar
Designer: Lellyn Creamer
Cover design: Nicole Bannister, Lellyn Creamer
Cartographers: Genené Hart, Nicole Bannister
Consultant: Neil Hewison
Picture Researcher: Shavonne Govender
Reproduction by Hirt & Carter (Pty) Ltd, Cape Town
Printed and bound by Times Offset (M) Sdn. Bhd.,
Malaysia.

Although every effort has been made to ensure
that this guide is up to date and current at time
of going to print, the Publisher accepts no
responsibility or liability for any loss, injury or
inconvenience incurred by readers or travellers
using this guide.

Photographic Credits:
Jon Arnold Images: pages 34, 35;
Axiom/James Morris: pages 8, 13, 14, 16, 17,
18, 21, 22, 27, 29, 36, 39 (top and bottom), 40,
41, 47, 51, 55, 63, 73, 78, 79; **Axiom/Dorian
Shaw:** page 74; **Robin Gauldie:** pages 9, 11,
28, 33, 52; **HL/Jeremy A. Horner:** page 24;
HL/Mary Jeliffe: page 72; **HL/Michael
Macintyre:** page 67; **HL/Liba Taylor:** page 76;
George B. Johnson: page 37; **Caroline Jones:**
page 62; **LF/Maggie Fagan:** page 43; **LF/Barry
Mayes:** pages 6, 83; **LF/Terry O'Brien:** pages
44, 50; **LF/Sue Wheat:** page 12; **James Morris**
pages 42, 64, 81; **PA:** page 38; **PB/Adrian
Baker:** title page; **PB/Jeanetta Baker:** page 82;
PB/Peter Baker: pages 10, 30, 32, 48; **PCL:**
front cover, pages 45, 49, 56, 66, 71, 84;
Mariëlle Renssen: pages 19, 20, 26; **Jeroen
Snijders:** pages 23, 25, 31; **Lawson Wood:**
pages 7, 15, 46, 65, 80.
*[HL: Hutchison Library; PB: PhotoBank;
LF: Life File; PA: Photo Access; PCL: Pictures
Colour Library]*

Front Cover: *The Great Pyramid and Sphinx.*
Title Page: *Arab village and people, West Bank*

CONTENTS

MAKE THE MOST OF YOUR GUIDE

Reading these two pages will help you to get the most out of your guide and save you time when using it. Sites discussed in the text are cross-referenced with the cover maps – for example, the reference 'Map A–C3' refers to the Cairo Map (Map A), column C, row 3. Use the Map Plan below to quickly locate the map you need.

MAP PLAN

Outside Back Cover

Outside Front Cover

Inside Front Cover

Inside Back Cover

THE BIGGER PICTURE

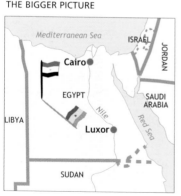

Key to Map Plan

A – Cairo
B – Pyramids of Giza
C – Pyramids of Saqqara
D – Alexandria
E – Valley of the Kings
F – Thebes Site
G – Luxor
H – Karnak
I – Temple of Luxor
J – Egypt
K – Around Cairo

USING THIS BOOK

Key to Symbols

⌧ — address   ⏰ — opening times

☎ — telephone   🚌 — tour

📠 — fax   💰 — entry fee

🖥 — website   🍴 — restaurants nearby

🖱 — e-mail address   **M** — nearest metro station

Map Legend

motorway		main road		Sharia el-Giza
national road		other road		Sharia Nubar
main road		metro		Ⓜ Sadat
minor road		built-up area		
railway		hotel		Ⓗ LONGCHAMPS
river	Nile	place of interest		★ Memphis
route number	2	building of interest		Cairo Opera House
city	CAIRO	university		◼
		museum		◿
major town	⊙ Giza	restaurant		Ⓡ
town	O Suez	embassy		⚑
large village	◎ Rosetta	post office		⌧
village	O Abu Simbel	parking area		P
oasis		tourist information		i
airport	✈ ✈	place of worship		△ Church △ Mosque
diving		police station		●
mountain peak	Mt Sinai ▲ 2285 m	bus terminus		🚌
		hospital		⊕
national park	Râs Muhammed National Park	park & garden		Zeinhum Gardens

Keep us Current

Travel information is apt to change, which is why we regularly update our guides. We'd be most grateful to receive feedback from you if you've noted something we should include in our updates. If you have any new information, please share it with us by writing to the Publishing Manager, Globetrotter, at the office nearest to you (addresses on the imprint page of this guide). The most significant contribution to each new edition will be rewarded with a free copy of the updated guide.

Above: *Dates are a staple crop in the desert oases and along the Nile.*
Opposite: *Masked butterfly fish are just one of the many species that can be seen on Egypt's teeming Red Sea reefs.*

The Desert
The desert begins on Cairo's doorstep, and the contrast between the vivid green of the irrigated farmland along the Nile near Luxor and the leafless sand only a few metres away is striking. Egypt has ambitious plans to divert water from the Nile to regions such as the New Valley – between Cairo and Luxor – creating more habitable land and easing Cairo's population burden.

CAIRO AND LUXOR

No city quite rivals **Cairo**'s exotic melange of ancient mystery, medieval romance and incredible urban sprawl. On the very edges of the modern city, seemingly about to be engulfed by a concrete and asphalt tide, the massive stone hulks of the pyramids have evoked awe in countless visitors since long before the dawn of European civilization. Yet these mighty tombs of generations of Pharaohs are only one aspect of Cairo's unique charisma, for this is a city on which many dynasties and cultures – Greek, Roman, Arab, Ottoman, even European – have left their mark, and modern Cairo is one of the most important cultural and political hubs of the Islamic world.

Luxor, on the banks of the Nile 720km (450 miles) south of the capital, is a welcome contrast from the thronged streets of the capital. It owes its existence almost entirely to the rediscovery, in the 19th century, of the richest array of ancient relics in Egypt: vast temple complexes and eerie underground tombs against a breathtaking backdrop of rocky desert hillsides. Life here moves more slowly, with white-turbaned drivers seeking passengers for their colourfully painted calèches (open horse-drawn carriages) along the Sharia Cornish el-Nil and white-sailed feluccas drifting along the Nile.

The Land
Climate

Cairo, Luxor and the Nile Valley are generally sunny and warm from November to March, with daytime temperatures around 20–24°C (68–75°F). Rain is rare at any time of year. From May to September temperatures can reach 35–40°C (95–104°F) and better-off Cairenes desert the stifling conditions of the capital for the more pleasant climate of the Mediterranean coast. If your main reason for going to Egypt is to see the sights of Cairo, Luxor and the Nile Valley, it would be unproductive to go in high summer.

Plant Life

Intensely urban Cairo and desert-fringed Luxor have few niches for wild flora and fauna. The fertile Nile Valley, intensively cultivated for more than 4000 years, is an almost entirely domesticated environment.

Date palms grows along the banks of the Nile even in city centres, as well as in courtyards and gardens. Among Cairo's few patches of urban greenery are Gezira Island, where palms grow in profusion, and the Zeinhum Gardens. **Papyrus reeds**, source of the first paper in the world, still grow along the Nile. Luxor is surrounded by the vivid greenery of cotton, sugar cane and lucerne (a type of clover), growing in a narrow, irrigated belt either side of the Nile which ends sharply at the desert's edge.

Wildlife

Bird life is abundant in the Nile Delta, which begins not far north of Cairo. White herons and cattle egrets can be seen fishing and roosting along the Nile, and pied kingfishers hover above the river. White and black storks appear on migration and red kites soar even in the skies of Cairo. Several species of vul-

> **The Nile**
> North of Cairo, the Nile divides into the two channels which form the **Nile Delta**, comprising hundreds of thousands of square kilometres of farmland, home to over 30 million people – 44 per cent of Egypt's total population. The world's longest river rises some 6690km (4160 miles) south of the Mediterranean coast, in the highlands of East Africa. Depositing fertile silt along its banks, it makes farming possible in a desert country that receives virtually no rainfall. Until 1971, with the completion of the High Dam at Aswan, the Nile flooded once a year along its entire length. The extent of the flood could spell prosperity or disaster for millions. Now, the waters of the Nile have been pent up to form **Lake Nasser**, a vast man-made reservoir that provides water year-round and supplies the entire country with hydroelectric power.

Akhenaten, Nefertiti and Tutankhamun
In the New Kingdom, Pharoah Akhenaten ditched the orthodox pantheon and decreed the cult of the sun-god Aten. He moved his capital from Luxor to Akhetaten, near modern Tell el-Amarna. Two famous archaeological finds ensure his place in history: the bust of his queen, Nefertiti, whose name became synonymous with female beauty, and the discovery of the tomb of his son and heir, Tutankhamun, who restored the old religion. Tutankhamun reigned for only seven years, dying at the age of 19 and bringing the royal line of the 18th Dynasty to an end, but his tomb was one of the few to survive the millennia unplundered by robbers, and yielded an amazing treasure trove.

ture, most commonly the Egyptian vulture, easily distinguished by its all-white plumage, may also be seen scavenging Cairo's gigantic rubbish dump. The hoopoe, with its striking crest, is often encountered along the roadsides. At dusk, bats are often seen fluttering among trees and along the river. Snakes are rare, but small gecko lizards can be spotted at night hunting for insects on lamplit walls.

History in Brief

Civilization has existed along the Nile Valley for so long that it makes Cairo seem relatively young. There were tool-using Neolithic communities here as early as 6000–7000BC. At some point between 3200 and 3000BC the first strong ruler of the Nile Valley, **Menes**, founded the first of the 30 dynasties which ruled Egypt for almost three millennia. For the next four centuries Menes and his successors of the 1st and 2nd Dynasties created and ruled the world's first great empire from their capital at **Memphis**, on the southern outskirts of present-day Cairo. The 3rd and 4th Dynasties (2686–2181BC) also ruled from Memphis, and they built vast tombs, temples and pyramids at Saqqara and Giza.

First Intermediate Period

Between 2200 and 2050BC, the Old Kingdom collapsed into a period of anarchy known as the First Intermediate Period which lasted until 2040BC.

The Middle Kingdom

Between 2160 and 2040BC the pharaohs of the 9th and 10th Dynasties established a monarchic rule based at

Below: *Hippos were among the most sacred animals of ancient Egypt.*

Heracleopolis near El-Faiyum, about 100km (62 miles) to the south of Cairo. They were ousted by the kings of the 11th Dynasty, whose Middle Kingdom spans the period of 2040–1782BC. Their first capital was at Thebes (Luxor), and they expanded their realm southward into Nubia.

Second Intermediate Period

Around 1782BC Egypt was invaded by the warlike Hyksos, from Asia Minor, whose chariots and bronze tools and weapons made them, at first, invincible. Settling in the Delta, they pushed south along the Nile. They were eventually driven out in 1570BC by the Theban ruler **Ahmose**, the founder of the 18th Dynasty, whose reign ushered in the era of the New Kingdom.

The New Kingdom

Under the 18th Dynasty, Luxor was the hub of an empire stretching from the fourth cataract of the Nile (in present-day Sudan) to the Euphrates River (in southwest Asia). Its rulers recorded their many feats in hieroglyphs at the Karnak temple complex, and **Hatshepsut** (1498–1483BC), one of the few women to rule Egypt in her own right, ordered the building of magnificent monuments on the West Bank of the Nile. A period of intermarriage between the pharaohs and the ruling families of the conquered Hittites and Mitanni (Medes) of Asia Minor followed the conquests of Tuthmosis III. The pharaohs then turned to projects like the Temple of Luxor, built by **Amenophis III** (1386–1349BC).

Above: *A statue of Tuthmosis at the Temple of Hatshepsut near Luxor.*

Pharaonic Egypt
The semi-divine pharaoh sat at the apex of a stable theocracy, wielding absolute temporal, military and religious power and making his will felt through a sophisticated civil service. The fertility of the Nile Valley let the Old Kingdom use its surplus labour to build great monuments to the pharaohs, such as the pyramids of Cheops, Chephren and Mycerinus at Giza, erected during the 4th Dynasty. Their complex theology was based on the sun, with a pantheon of deities concerned with every aspect of life and death.

Above: *The face of Tutankhamun, perhaps the best-known pharaoh of all.*

Decline and Fall

Ramses III, founder of the 20th Dynasty in 1195BC, is best known for victories over a series of invaders, but the records show Egypt assailed on all sides by attackers who found the empire weakened by a power struggle between the pharaohs and the hereditary high priests. Between the end of the 20th Dynasty in 1090BC and the advent of Alexander in 332BC, few dynasties lasted more than 150 years. Nubian kings conquered the empire, only for their capital at Thebes (Luxor) to be pillaged by Assyrian invaders. By the beginning of the 5th century BC Egypt had been conquered by Persia.

The Romans

Egypt was added to the Roman Empire in 30BC, remaining a Roman province for the next seven centuries. Christianity was introduced by St Mark in AD45. With the partition of the Empire into east and west in AD379, Egypt came under the rule of Constantinople, capital of the eastern Empire (Byzantium).

The Age of Saladin

In 1079, the Crusaders landed in Palestine to drive the Muslims out of the Holy Land and recapture Jerusalem for Christendom. They set up a chain of petty kingdoms and expanded steadily, capturing Jerusalem in 1099. By the mid-12th century they threatened Egypt, but were defeated by the Kurdish general Salah el-Din (Saladin). Jerusalem was recaptured in 1187 and the Crusader kingdoms reconquered. Saladin went on to make himself ruler of Egypt, fortifying Cairo and building the massive Citadel which still stands in the old city.

HISTORY IN BRIEF

The Mamelukes

Cairo was the seat of Saladin's heirs until 1250 when the throne passed to **Aybak**, chief of the Mamelukes, an elite corps of soldier-slaves who ruled Egypt for the next 267 years. The reign of the Mamelukes was harsh, corrupt and marked by treachery and deceit.

The Ottoman Empire

Turkish Sultan **Suleiman the Magnificent** found Egypt an easy conquest in 1517, with the Mamelukes unable to unite against him. For the next three centuries, Egypt belonged to an Ottoman Empire stretching from the Red Sea to the Danube. Its provincial governors (pashas) were appointed by the Sultan in Constantinople. Cairo was already a centre of Islamic learning, the Islamic university of Al-Azhar having been founded in 971.

The French

A French Revolutionary force under Bonaparte (*see* panel, page 13) landed in Egypt in 1798. Its main aim was to control the strategic route to India via Suez. Advancing as far as Cairo (where his gunners are blamed for blowing the nose off the Sphinx while using it for target practice), Napoleon was cut off from France when Nelson's ships sank the French fleet at Aboukir Bay (near the western mouth of the Nile). In 1801 the remnants of the French expedition withdrew.

The Co-Dominium

Throughout the 19th century, Cairo (though still the capital of the country) remained in the shadow of Alexandria, the port that was Egypt's gateway to Europe and dominated economic and commercial life.

> **The Coming of Islam**
> The coming of Islam was rapid and unexpected. Cairo fell to the Muslim Arabs in 641, and for the next two centuries, the Muslim Emirs of Egypt were vassals of the Abbassid Caliphate of Baghdad, then the capital of the Islamic world. In 969 the Fatimid Caliphs of Kairouan (in modern Tunisia) conquered Egypt and founded a new city on the banks of the Nile as their capital; they named it El-Qahira (the victorious). Cairo quickly became one of the most important political, religious and cultural centres of the Islamic world.

Below: *Minarets such as this one at Luxor dominate the skylines of virtually every Egyptian town.*

Mohammed Ali Pasha

The French invasion freed Egypt from Ottoman rule and opened a window to the West, encouraging some Egyptians to seek reform. Supported by his soldiers, a charismatic army officer of Greek-Albanian birth, Mohammed Ali, declared himself Pasha of Egypt. While paying lip service to the Ottoman Sultan, he ruled Egypt for 40 years, instituting a programme of modernization. His successors, ruling with the title of Khedive, did not even pretend to be vassals of the crumbling Ottoman Empire.

Below: *Allied and Axis war dead are commemorated at the cemeteries of El-Alamein.*

As the European influence on Egypt grew, Alexandria became even more important.

The French engineer Ferdinand de Lesseps pioneered the **Suez Canal**, which opened in 1869, providing Europe with a quicker sea route to India and the Far East. The incompetent Khedive Ismail sold Egypt's 44 per cent holding in the canal to British and French financiers. In 1876, a Franco-British 'co-dominium' was set up to manage the khedive's affairs, and in 1882 Britain sent a garrison to Alexandria. Locked in imperial rivalry with France, Britain tightened its hold, making Egypt a *de facto* protectorate.

Now began the era of the Egyptologists. At first they were little more than gangs of adventurers and tomb-raiders, more interested in the treasures of the pharaohs than in what they might reveal about Egypt's ancient cultures. Founding the Institute of Archaeology in Cairo in 1880 helped to bring about a more scientific approach.

Egypt formally became a British protectorate in 1914, but then in 1922 it regained its independence, though Britain kept control of defence and of the Suez Canal.

World War II

The Suez Canal was vital to the Allied war effort. Egypt was invaded first by Italian forces, then, after the Allied defeat of the Italians, by Rommel's German Afrika Korps. In November 1942 the decisive Allied victory at **El-Alamein**, only 106km (66 miles) west of Alexandria, turned the tide.

The Birth of Modern Egypt

In 1945 Egypt was a founder of the Arab League. In 1948 it was drawn into the first

Above: *The High Dam at Aswan, an enduring monument to strongman Gamal Abdel Nasser.*

Arab-Israeli war, when the Arab states attempted to snuff out the newly formed State of Israel. Defeat increased discontent with the incompetent and extravagant rule of King Farouk, who had come to the throne in 1936. In July 1952 the last of Mohammed Ali's line was overthrown by an army junta dominated by **Gamal Abdel Nasser** (*see* panel, page 14), and in June 1953 Egypt was declared a republic. Nasser began a programme of nationalization which culminated in the unilateral nationalizing of the Suez Canal, provoking a combined British, French and Israeli invasion which failed after an American ultimatum forced the invaders to withdraw.

Nasser's successor, **Anwar Sadat**, moved Egypt closer to the West. His assault on Israel in the 'Yom Kippur War' of October 1973, though it failed to drive the Israelis out of Sinai, helped restore Egypt's self-esteem after the defeat of 1967 and helped Sadat to begin a peace process with Israel in 1977. With the Camp David agreement of 1979, Israel withdrew from Sinai to its 1967 border with Egypt. Sadat was assassinated by Egyptian Muslim extremists in 1981.

President **Hosni Mubarak** has continued Sadat's policy of *rapprochement* with the West. During the Gulf War of 1991 Egypt was a supporter of the US-led alliance against Iraq. Extreme Islamists carried out a campaign of terror in the mid-1990s and in 1997 58 tourists were gunned down by terrorists at the Temple of Hatshepsut in Luxor. Egyptian extremists have also been associated with the Al-Qaeda terrorist movement.

Napoleon's Scholars
The French expedition was more than a military adventure. Napoleon's infantry carved their names into the ancient stones, but Bonaparte also brought a team of scholars who were the first to reveal Egypt's ancient wonders, including the **Rosetta Stone** (which eventually allowed the deciphering of the ancient hieroglyphs), to the world.

Above: *Nowadays younger Egyptians are deserting the Delta villages for the streets of Cairo and other cities.*

Gamal Abdel Nasser
Nasser became a hero to the Arab world overnight after humiliating Israel, France and Britain. He flirted with the Soviet Union, acquiring Soviet weaponry and welcoming military and technical advisers from the USSR. Soviet aid and expertise built the **Aswan High Dam**, Nasser's most enduring monument, which was completed a year after his death in 1971. Nasser's heroic status survived even the shattering defeat of the Six Day War in 1967, when Israel shattered Arab forces poised on its borders and seized Sinai from Egypt.

Government and Economy

Egypt is in theory a democracy, but despite the presence of several small opposition parties in the People's Assembly (the country's parliament), the ruling **National Democratic Party** has no real rival for power.

The head of state and the real political power is the president, elected for a six-year term (Mubarak was re-elected to a fifth term in 2005), who is also chief of the armed forces and appoints the vice president, prime minister, regional governors, police chiefs and other key officials. Much legislation is by presidential decree, and there is no effective system of political and judicial checks and balances. The two-chamber parliament consists of an appointed **Consultative Assembly**, which has no legislative role, and the **People's Assembly**, a legislative body elected by universal suffrage every five years.

Since the 1980s, the government has pursued a more liberal economic policy, easing currency controls and restrictions on private capital, encouraging inward investment and recognizing that the free market is likely to be more effective than a command economy.

The People

Cairo is home to at least 15 million, perhaps as many as 20 million, of Egypt's approximately 75 million people. The drift to the capital has snowballed over the last three decades, with younger people – especially young men – quitting low-paid jobs in agricultural villages for the bright lights of Cairo. A high birth rate and a higher life expectancy, thanks to cleaner water, better diet and improved health care, also swell the city's population. National population growth is at present around 1.33 million a year, with potentially disastrous results.

Urban Egyptians share the preoccupations of city-dwellers the world over, and thanks to the Internet and satellite TV, Cairo-dwellers are aware of the rest of the world as never before. In **rural villages** outside the capital, and only a few hundred metres from the tourist sights of Luxor, however, life still proceeds at a much more traditional pace. Most people rise at dawn, and the donkey, ox-cart and sailing felucca are still more important means of transport than the pick-up truck. Any village worth the name has its mosque, and the call to prayer sets the daily rhythm. But modern road, rail and air transport means that, for village youths, the temptations of the city are never very far away.

Language

Spoken **Egyptian Arabic** differs considerably from, for example, Moroccan Arabic, but the written form of the language is identical across the Arabic-speaking world. Arabic script reads from right to left, and uses 29 letters. It is not always possible to transcribe Arabic letters exactly into English: the guttural sounds represented as Q, Kh, Gh, ' and ` present particular problems, and short vowels are not written. On maps and in local guides you may find place names spelt in several different ways (for instance Qena/Kena, Edfu/Idfu, Saqqara/Sakkara). Use your imagination.

> **Tourism**
> Tourism is an important foreign currency earner in Egypt, especially in areas like Luxor which have attracted well-heeled European sight-seers since the 19th century. A downturn in tourism after the Luxor massacre of 1997 was followed by a quick recovery in visitor numbers. The attacks on Taba in 2004 and Sharm el Sheikh in 2005 were bloody, but deterred tourists only temporarily.

Below: *Bedouin desert wanderers are gradually being forced to give up their traditional way of life.*

Egyptians are aware of a distinct national identity, and Cairenes are proud of a **cosmopolitan** outlook formed by many different cultures. Until the upsurge of nationalism under Nasser, **French** was the second language of the educated professional class, while under the British protectorate **English** was added to the linguistic portfolio. Almost everyone involved in tourism, from camel-men and felucca skippers to the management of luxury hotels, can speak and understand a bit of English and French, German and Italian as well. However, any attempt on your part to communicate in Arabic will always be warmly welcomed by your Egyptian hosts (*see* Useful Phrases, page 91).

Religion

Islam is the official faith, and Egyptians tend to be devout without being fanatical about it. The 1000-year-old El-Azhar University in Cairo (*see* page 24) is one of the

guiding lights of the (Sunni) Islamic world. Egyptian society as a whole takes a relaxed view of some of Islam's more onerous prohibitions, and that is especially true in cosmopolitan Cairo and in tourism-dependent Luxor.

During the great Islamic festivals, however, Egypt is more visibly Muslim. During **Ramadan**, the month when good Muslims fast from dawn until dusk, some hotel bars are reluctant to serve alcohol, and the restaurants and cafés outside of the large hotels will be even more

THE PEOPLE

severely curtailed. To compensate, the festival of **Eid el-Fitr**, at the end of Ramadan, is marked by feasting, fireworks, and colourful open-air celebrations.

About 90 per cent of the population of the country is Muslim. Most of the rest are **Coptic Christians**, whose faith was brought to Egypt by St Mark. The Coptic church split from Orthodox Christianity in AD451, and the Islamic conquest made its isolation complete. Several historic churches survive in Cairo, but the monasteries of the Western Desert (such as Deir el Baramous, Deir el Suriani, and Deir Abu Maqar, midway between Cairo and Alexandria) are the heart of the Coptic tradition.

Art and Culture

The painters of the pharaonic ages, whose work illuminates the walls of millennia-old tombs, had a marvellous grasp of line and colour, while their skill in blending pigments means that their paintings today are almost as vivid as the day they were painted. Even more impressive are the technical abilities of the architects and builders of the ancient world, whose achievements – most of all the mighty pyramids of Giza – still have the power to astonish. During the Ptolemaic era, Hellenistic influences crept into Egyptian monumental architecture, most notably along the Nile south of Luxor in temples such as those built by the Ptolemies at Edfu, Esna or Kom Ombo.

Above: *In Nubia, south of Aswan, village life has changed very little.*
Opposite: *The tomb of a Mameluke princess, Khawand Tatar el-Higaziya.*

Islamic Architecture and Design
Islam's influence on Cairene architecture is most evident within the city's great mosques and madrasas (religious colleges), dating mostly from the Mameluke era. Islam bans representational art, but in Egypt (as elsewhere in the Muslim world) a rich decorative style has evolved, featuring graceful calligraphy from the Koran and complex geometric patterns. Mosques dating from the Ottoman era are notable for their slim, columnar minarets, which appear much more graceful than the shorter, more massive towers of earlier mosques.

HIGHLIGHTS

Egyptian Antiquities Museum
⊕ 09:00–18:45 daily,
closed Fri 11:15–13:30
✉ Midan el-Tahrir
☎ (02) 578 2852
📠 (02) 579 4596
🖥 www.
egyptianmuseum.gov.eg
🛈 E£50 for museum
only; E£100 extra to get
into the Mummy Room
🍴 Midan Tahrir
⊕ 09:00–16:30 daily

**Pyramids of Giza
and the Sphinx**
⊕ 08:00–16:00 daily
✉ Pyramid Road,
18km (11 miles) south-
west of central Cairo
🛈 E£50

Below: *Relics of the
Old Kingdom at the
Antiquities Museum.*

🌀 *See* Map A–C3 | ★★★

EGYPTIAN ANTIQUITIES MUSEUM

The Egyptian Antiquities Service, founded in 1835, was the first attempt to curb the looting of ancient tombs and temples by treasure-hunters, and to create a national collection of archaeological finds. In 1858, the newly appointed director, **Auguste Mariette**, created the first national museum. Its site at Boulaq was subject to flooding and it was moved, first to Ismail Pasha's palace at Giza, then, in 1904, to its present site, north of Midan el-Tahrir (Liberation Square) in the centre of Cairo. Crammed with over a century's worth of finds – more than 120,000 objects – the museum is perhaps the world's greatest archaeological collection, and the logical first stop on any visit to Cairo. There are more than 50 galleries, and a clockwise tour of the museum leads you from relics of the Old Kingdom on the ground floor, through the Middle and New Kingdoms, and finally to the Hellenistic-Roman era of the Ptolemies and Caesars. The tour reaches a crescendo on the first floor, where the **Tutankhamun galleries** house an unbelievable wealth of finds from the boy-pharaoh's tomb – the only tomb so far to be found completely unplundered by treasure-seekers. The bodies of **Ramses II** and some other less renowned pharaohs can be seen in the Mummy Room.

See Maps B, J–C2   ★★★

GREAT PYRAMIDS OF GIZA

Giza, 11km (7 miles) southwest of the city centre, has become a suburb of Cairo, spreading up to the foot of the desert plateau so that the Great Pyramids no longer stand, splendid and enigmatic, amid trackless sand. The inspiration of scores of hypotheses, the pyramids are the ultimate symbol of ancient Egypt. They were originally surfaced in polished limestone, which can still be seen in places, and so were considerably less rugged than they now appear. The three main pyramids of the Giza complex are by no means the earliest – that honour goes to the pyramid built by the 3rd Dynasty pharaoh Zoser at Saqqara – but are by far the most impressive.

Above: *The Pyramid of Chephren still has much of its polished limestone cladding.*

The largest, the **Great Pyramid of Cheops** (2551–2528BC), is built of an estimated 2.5 million blocks, rising to a 137m (450ft) summit. Inside it, the **Great Gallery** leads to the **King's Chamber**. Originally full of treasures and goods to accompany the king on his journey into the afterlife, this is now a dank and empty cavern occupied only by an empty sarcophagus – an anti-climax after the awesome exterior and the scarily claustrophobic journey to the centre of the pyramid. Almost as large as Cheops's pile, the 136m (446ft) **Pyramid of Chephren** (2520–2494BC) has kept the limestone cladding its peak, and because it is on slightly higher ground looks taller than its neighbour. Like that of Cheops, it is empty, as is the smaller, 66m (217ft) **Pyramid of Mycerinus** (2490–2472BC), opened by British archaeologists in 1817. The stone sarcophagus they found within was lost when the ship carrying it back to Britain sank.

> **Making Mummies**
> Ancient Egyptians believed the survival after death of the *ka*, or spirit, depended on preservation of the body. Mummification was a highly developed skill, and the process took up to two months. The soft organs were removed and stored in separate containers, known as **Canopic jars**. The heart, which was believed to be the seat of the soul, was left in place. After five weeks' pickling in natron, a dehydrating agent, the body was stuffed with a mixture of clay, resin and sawdust, coated with fragrant ointments, and wrapped in resin-soaked bandages before being placed in its painted sarcophagus.

HIGHLIGHTS

⚙ *See* Map J–D2   ★★★

Right: *The Sphinx re-emerged anew in 1998 from a painstaking restoration programme.*

THE SPHINX

As symbolic of Egypt as the Pyramids, the Sphinx was probably commissioned by Chephren, son of Cheops, whose pyramid is nearby. Sculpted from one huge block of limestone, the colossal figure has the body of a lion and the serene head of a god or demi-god, modelled on Chephren himself.

Standing some 20m (66ft) high, the Sphinx shows the marks of time: the rock is heavily eroded, the facial features were chiselled away by devout Muslims in the 14th century, and both Turkish and French gunners used it for target practice – the Turks shot off its beard, which is now in the British Museum in London, and the French blew off the nose. Blocks from its left shoulder crumbled away in 1988, prompting an emergency repair programme which was completed in 1998 – the latest in a series of repairs first begun under the Ptolemies over 2000 years ago, some of which did as much harm as good.

The Sphinx was worshipped as an avatar of the sun-god Horus.

Restoring the Sphinx
In 1998, restoration experts completed a ten-year project to repair the Sphinx, which had been badly damaged by thousands of years of erosion, vandalism and more recently air pollution – but also by misguided earlier efforts at restoration. (Blocks from the statue's left shoulder fell away in 1988.) The purpose of the man-headed, lion-bodied statue still puzzles archaeologists, but the human head is thought to symbolize intelligence while the leonine body stands for power and kingship.

See Map A–E4/F4 ★★★

CITADEL OF SALADIN

The heart of medieval Cairo is the complex of hilltop battlements and bastions begun by Saladin in 1176. Seat of the rulers of Egypt until the mid-19th century, it is one of the city's main landmarks, rising above the old bazaar area. Within the walls, the **Mohammed Ali Mosque**, known as the **Alabaster Mosque**, is crowned by a huge central dome, ringed by slender minarets and supporting half-domes, dominating the Citadel and medieval Cairo below it. Begun in 1830 by Egypt's first modernizing ruler, Mohammed Ali Pasha, it was completed in 1848; he is buried inside. Adorned by verses from the *Koran* in delicate Arabic calligraphy and by complex geometric patterns, the interior of this massive building is surprisingly light and airy. In the southern part of the citadel, the **El-Gawhara Palace** (the Palace of Mohammed Ali) was built for the Pasha in 1814. Within are portraits of supercilious 19th-century pashas, dusty costumes and gilt and plush furniture. In the northern sector, the Harim Palace – originally Mohammed Ali's private residence – houses the **Military Museum**, a collection of photographs, documents and musical instruments, while the state carriages of Egyptian royalty are on display in the nearby **Carriage Museum**. Also nearby is the **National Police Museum**, which contains a rogues' gallery of Egypt's most notorious criminals. It is worth ascending the parapets of the Citadel, behind the National Police Museum, for a panoramic view of medieval Cairo and its historic mosques.

The Citadel of Saladin
🕐 08:00–16:00 daily
✉ Sharia Salah Salim
☎ (02) 512 1735
💰 E£50

Below: *The Mosque of Mohammed Ali dominates the medieval Citadel.*

HIGHLIGHTS

Khan el-Khalili Bazaar
🕐 open 24 hours; shops generally open 10:00–20:00; most are closed on Sunday
✉ Khan el-Khalili
💰 free

🌐 *See Map A–F3* | ★★★

KHAN EL-KHALILI BAZAAR

In many ways, the labyrinth of narrow streets which is Khan el-Khalili is the real heart of Cairo, throbbing to a steady beat from dawn until after midnight. Far more than a tourist attraction, the bazaar first opened for business in 1382 and has been hustling and bustling ever since. Like all true Middle Eastern bazaar districts, it is far more than a shopping precinct, for it is also home to thousands of Cairenes. When your feet tire of pounding its pavements you can join them for a nargileh (water pipe) of apple-flavoured tobacco and a glass of coffee perfumed with cardamom in one of the scores of coffee houses hidden away in its pungently scented lanes and alleys, where the smell of spices, perfumes, charcoal smoke and freshly tanned leather wafts in a complex aroma. Things to buy range from water pipes and brassware to rugs and carpets, antique furniture and musical instruments, all on sale alongside herbs, spices, fresh fruit and vegetables and more mundane modern house-hold goods. Allow yourself plenty of time to explore this maze of shopping streets, because you will inevitably and irresistibly be ushered into more than one shop to examine its stock in trade, and bargaining over purchases is a lengthy and leisurely procedure. Getting lost, too, is almost inevitable, but shopkeepers and other locals are usually happy to help you regain your bearings. (*See also* page 53.)

Below: *Almost anything can be bought from the bazaar stalls, but haggling is de rigueur.*

See Map A–D4/E4 ★★★

Above: *The 9th-century Mosque of Ibn Tulun is architecturally unique and is the oldest mosque still in use in the city.*

IBN TULUN MOSQUE

One of the largest mosques in the world, this spectacular 9th-century edifice is one of the most striking pieces of Islamic architecture in Cairo. Thousands gather weekly to pray in its vast central courtyard, and its tall minaret is unique in having an external spiral stair. **Ahmed ibn Tulun**, the Turkish governor who founded it, declared his independence from the Ottoman Sultan in Constantinople in the late 9th century.

The mosque, which was rebuilt in its present form in 1297 by **Sultan Lagin**, has the pilasters and slightly pointed arches typical of the Abbasid style of Islamic religious architecture, but also borrows details from the architecture of Muslim Baghdad and from Coptic Christian design.

Next to the mosque's outer courtyard is the **Gayer-Anderson Museum**, which is housed in two medieval houses. It was founded by an early 20th-century English resident and houses a collection of Oriental furniture and antiques.

Ibn Tulun Mosque
⊠ Sharia el-Saliba/ Sharia Tulun, west of the Citadel
🕘 08:00–16:00 daily except Fri prayers
🔆 free

Gayer-Anderson Museum
⊠ next to the Ibn Tulun Mosque
☎ (02) 364 7822
🕘 08:00–16:00 daily except Fri prayers
🔆 E£30

Above: *View of the El-Azhar Mosque, one of the Islamic world's great centres of learning.*

 See Map A–F3 ★★★

EL-AZHAR MOSQUE AND UNIVERSITY

The El-Azhar Mosque, which was completed in AD971 (and thus predates almost every other centre of learning in the world), is one of the beacons of Islam. The leading intellectual centre of orthodox Sunni Islam, it is both a mosque and theological university, and for more than 1000 years it has wielded enormous influence across the entire Muslim world. With a student body of more than 20,000, it attracts scholars not only from Egypt but from all its Arab neighbours and from Muslim nations as diverse as Indonesia and Malaysia in the east and Mauretania and Morocco in the west. El-Azhar also draws its students from Muslim communities in Europe, East and Southern Africa and North America, and perhaps more than at any time in its past, with Islam at a historic cross-roads, is a hothouse of ideas and religious debate. Foreign students receive free lodging, and many are the beneficiaries of scholarships endowed centuries ago by devout Muslim philanthropists.

Many of Cairo's rulers – each trying to outdo his predecessors – endowed El-Azhar with new buildings and faculties. In addition to its venerable Koranic schools, its fields of study have more recently been expanded to include medicine and science. The *Koran*, however, is still studied, as it has been for centuries, among the columns of the central court, where scholars of Islam sit cross-legged around their teachers.

El-Azhar Mosque and University
🕐 daily, except to non-Muslims during Muslim prayers
✉ Sharia el-Azhar
🖥 www.alazhar.org
💰 free

EL-AZHAR & COPTIC MUSEUM

See Map A–C6   ★★★

COPTIC MUSEUM AND ROMAN WALLS

The Misr el-Qadima quarter, close to the Nile and south of the city centre, is the heart of Coptic Cairo, with numerous surviving Coptic churches. The Coptic Museum's collection contains relics of Christianity's heyday in Egypt, during the later centuries of the Roman Empire, including icons and religious paintings, tapestries, manuscripts and carvings. These provide fascinating evidence of links to a pre-Christian past. There is a clear artistic continuity between the Egypt of the pharaohs and the later Christian world – even the Egyptian ankh or looped cross, the symbol of life, may have influenced Christian symbolism. Coptic art reached its zenith from the 5th–7th centuries AD, in the era between Coptic Christianity's rift with the orthodox Church until the coming of Islam.

Part of the museum encloses the twin gate-towers which are all that remain of the walled stronghold built by the Romans and demolished in the 19th century. The gate once opened directly onto the Nile (which has since shifted its course) and was part of the fortifications built by Octavian (later Augustus Caesar) to secure his control of Egypt after defeating Cleopatra and her lover Mark Anthony.

Coptic Museum
🕑 daily 09:00–17:00
✉ Sharia Mari Girgis
☎ (02) 363 9742
💻 www.copticmuseum.gov.eg
Ⓜ Mar Girgis
💰 E£30
🍽 cafeteria, open 09:00–17:00

Roman Walls
Visitor information the same as for the Coptic Museum.

Below: *The Coptic Museum, with its arched entrance and carved stonework, contains relics of Egypt's Christian heritage and evidence of links to a pre-Christian past.*

Saqqara
🕐 sites open
08:00–16:00 daily
✉ Saqqara
💲 E£50

Imhotep Museum
🕐 09:00–16:00
💲 E£20

See Maps C, J–D2 ★★★

SAQQARA

The earliest and most important relic among the pyramids of Saqqara, 30km (19 miles) south of Cairo, is the **Step Pyramid of Zoser**, which dates from 2650BC and thus precedes the Giza complex by about a century. The earliest type of pyramid, it takes the form of a tiered stack of square *mastabas* (chambered tombs), and was designed by Imhotep, first of the great architects of the pharaohs. His design inspired later builders, who found a way of achieving a regular finish by cladding the stepped limestone blocks with polished limestone. Zoser's pyramid stands at the heart of a large necropolis, surrounded by walls and courtyards decorated with friezes boasting of the pharaoh's feats and victories.

A few hundred metres to the southwest, the **Pyramid of Unas** looks dilapidated, but its crumbling exterior conceals inner walls covered in heiroglyphs inspired by the cult of Osiris, which reached its zenith during the reign of Unas, last pharaoh of the 5th Dynasty. Near the site entrance, the new **Imhotep Museum**, opened in 2006, is an impressive showcase for some of the wonderful discoveries made at Saqqara. The main hall houses reconstructions of some of the architectural elements of the site, while other halls display new discoveries, including statues, mummies, and bronze surgical tools from the tomb of a dentist.

Below: *The Step Pyramid of Zoser was built more than 4500 years ago.*

See Map J–D2 ★★★

MEMPHIS

Memphis, strategically placed between the Nile Valley and its Delta, around 32km (20 miles) south of Cairo, is a key landmark in Egyptian history. This is where the pharaonic dynasties began, with the unification of Upper and Lower Egypt by Menes. Even after the pharaohs of the New Kingdom moved their imperial capital to Luxor, it remained the most important city in lower Egypt until the advent of the Ptolemies, who founded, and ruled from, the city of Alexandria on the Mediterranean coast.

Above: *This colossal statue can be seen at the Memphis Museum.*

Sadly, what remains to be seen of the world's first great imperial city is less impressive than its history suggests. The Nile mud has reclaimed most of the ancient mud-brick buildings, while many of the stone buildings were demolished to provide ready-dressed stone for the building of medieval Cairo. Much of the site on which the city stood is now covered by fields. That said, the open-air on-site **Museum**, with its collection of stelae and statues surrounding a viewing gallery which contains a prone colossus of Rameses II, is well worth a look. Next to it are the stone trenches of mummification beds, used to prepare the sacred Bulls of Apis for mummification and burial in the Serapeum at Saqqara (*see* page 26).

Memphis is hardly worth a visit in its own right, but is worth seeing in combination with the more impressive ruins of Saqqara, only 6km (3.5 miles) away.

Memphis
🕐 site and museum
08:00–16:00 daily
✉ Memphis
💰 E£35

Above: *The massive Temple of Karnak complex is the highlight of any visit to Luxor.*

Temple of Karnak
🕐 daily 06:00–17:30 winter, 06:00–18:30 summer; sound and light shows 18:30, 19:45, 21:00 and 22:15 in winter, one hour later in summer
🚌 microbuses along Cornish el-Nil from town centre
💰 E£50, Sound and Light Show E£55
💻 www.egyptsandl.com

Valley of the Kings
🕐 daily 08:00–17:30 in winter, 07:00–18:30 in summer
✉ West Bank, Thebes
💰 E£70 (main site and three tombs), E£80 (Tomb of Tutankhamun)

See Maps H, J–E4	★★★

TEMPLE OF KARNAK

The height of enormity in terms of time as well as space – it is the largest known temple complex in the world – Karnak is the most thrilling part of any visit to Luxor. Begun in the Middle Kingdom, it was still being added to during the 25th Dynasty, 1300 years later. Dedicated to Amun, greatest of Egyptian gods, Karnak was the spiritual centre of the kingdom, and the temple and its priests were a great power in the land, controlling great estates and vast numbers of slaves and workers.

Most visitors spend no more than half a day or less at Karnak, but it really takes several days to take in the whole complex, in even superficial detail, and it is well worth visiting Karnak at least twice: once during the day, when you can see the scope and plan of the complex and look at its intricate and detailed inscriptions and murals, and a second time in the evening for the excellent Sound and Light Show.

Ranks of ram-headed sphinxes line a processional avenue leading to a towering gateway, through walls that stand almost 45m (147ft) high. Within the Great Court is the **Temple of Ramses III**. Two colossi of Ramses II guard the way into the Great Hypostyle Hall, a 6000m² (7176 sq yd) space cluttered with vast pillars, and two more gateways lead you to the oldest section of the temple complex and the 29.2m (95.8ft) Obelisk of Hatshepsut. Beyond is the Wall of Records, where inscriptions relate the triumphs of Tuthmosis II.

KARNAK & VALLEY OF THE KINGS

🌸 See Maps E, F–A1/B2 ★★★

VALLEY OF THE KINGS

The Valley of the Kings at first sight appears unimpressive, but buried deep in the hillsides of this desolate, sun-baked valley are the tombs of more than 60 kings. Despite the elaborate precautions they took to hide their treasures from tomb-robbers, only a single tomb – that of the boy-king **Tutankhamun** – has ever been found intact. Tutakhamun's tomb is an obligatory stop, but a sad anticlimax – its treasures are all in the Egyptian Antiquities Museum (*see* page 18), leaving only a small, empty stone chamber. Many more tombs are equally anticlimactic. Some of them are no more than tunnels in which a few scraps of painting or relief are the only indication of their antiquity. The most impressive tomb is that of **Seti I**, a deep tunnel which plunges 100m (109yd) into the rock. Its reliefs are in excellent condition, and the ceiling is decorated with sacred texts and sacred vultures. Fine murals also decorate the entrance to the **Tomb of Seti II**.

Also worth seeing is the **Tomb of Ramses VI**, which reaches 83m (90yd) into the hillside and is decorated with illustrations of the Egyptian sacred texts, the *Book of the Dead*, the *Book of the Caverns* and the *Book of Gates*.

> **Howard Carter**
> British archaeologist Howard Carter spent six years digging in the Valley of the Kings before his conviction that it held the secret of Tutankhamun's tomb was proved right in 1922, when he found first a flight of steps, then the sealed door of the tomb. Within he found, according to his own account '…strange animals, statuary and gold – everywhere the glint of gold … I was struck dumb with amazement.'

Below: *In the tomb of Ramses VI, these colourful paintings depict various scenes from the* Book of the Dead.

Temple of Luxor
🕐 daily 08:00–21:00 in winter, 08:00–22:00 in summer; the temple is floodlit at night
✉ Sharia Cornish el-Nil
💰 E£40

Mosque of Abul-Haggag
✉ entrance from Sharia el-Karnak, behind the Temple of Luxor

⭐ See Maps I, G–A4/B4 ★★★

TEMPLE OF LUXOR

The most obvious landmark in Luxor is this magnificent complex of columns, statues and sphinxes, which lay buried beneath the mud dwellings until archaeological excavations began in the 19th century. The temple is situated in the town centre, close to the Nile and incongruously adjacent to the golden arches of Luxor's branch of a well-known American burger chain.

Two gigantic statues of **Ramses II** stand guard in front of the mighty stone pylons (ceremonial gateposts) marking the temple entrance. Within, there are more colossi of Ramses and his queen, **Nefertari**, and the **Court** and **Colonnade of Amenophis III**, the 18th-Dynasty Pharaoh who built much of the temple. An avenue of small sphinxes leads north from the entrance, all that remains of a stone-paved processional way which in ancient times connected the Temple of Luxor with the temples of **Karnak**, almost 5km (3 miles) to the north. A much later addition to the temple complex is the

Below: *Crouching sphinxes along the processional avenue at Luxor.*

Mosque of Abul-Haggag, which perches atop the inner court of the temple. Faced with patterned yellow and blue tiles, the mosque makes a colourful contrast to the monochrome walls and columns which surround it. Dating from the 13th century, it commemorates a local sheikh and is still in daily use by worshippers.

Temple of Luxor & Luxor Museum

See Map G–B3 ★★

LUXOR MUSEUM

This superb museum is second only to the Egyptian Antiquities Museum in terms of the wealth of its magnificent collection of finds from some of Egypt's richest sources of ancient artefacts. Opened in 1975, it is also much more modern (and usually less crowded) than its Cairo rival, and its clearer layout makes its treasures all the more fascinating and informative. Among its most impressive exhibits are the collection of pink granite and black basalt statues of pharaohs from many dynasties. These were rediscovered in 1989 at a site within the central court of the **Temple of Luxor**, and are believed to have been buried at some time during the Roman period – perhaps to prevent them from being seized and taken to Rome. Some seem grim and authoritarian, while others smile serenely, secure in their power.

Finds from the **Tomb of Tutankhamun** (most of whose treasures are in the National Antiquities Museum) include a superbly preserved golden cow's head, a royal bed, and model ships intended to transport the pharaoh to the world of the dead. In the upper gallery is a reconstruction of one of the friezes from the shrines built at Karnak by Akhenaten, which were later demolished for use in the ceremonial gateways to the Karnak complex built during the reign of Ramses II. The museum also has a fine array of exhibits from Ptolemaic and Roman times, including coins, jewellery, tiny bronze and clay figurines and elegant glassware.

Above: *The Luxor Museum's collection of finds from Luxor, Karnak and Thebes has few rivals.*

Anubis
With the head of a jackal and the body of a man, Anubis was the Egyptian god of death, who judged each Egyptian after his death, weighing his heart against the feather of truth. He was also the god of embalming and mummification, and his black skin symbolized the fertile black mud of the Nile.

Luxor Museum
🕐 daily 09:00–13:00 and 16:00–21:00 in winter, 09:00–13:00 and 17:00–22:00 in summer
✉ Sharia Cornish el-Nil
💰 E£70

Below: *The Temple of Hatshepsut, on the Nile's west bank.*

 See Maps E, F–B2 | ★★

TEMPLE OF HATSHEPSUT

Hatshepsut, daughter of the 18th-Dynasty ruler **Tuthmosis I**, was one of the few women to rule Egypt in her own right, though her statues depict her wearing the ceremonial false chin-beard of a male pharaoh in token of her rank. Her mortuary temple, standing alone, seems to grow out of the towering pink cliffs into which it was built. Within its colonnades, superbly detailed reliefs depict her peaceful expansion of the empire's trade links through the Red Sea with the African kingdom of Punt (modern Somalia). These friezes seem almost like a modern documentary. The superbly realistic portrayals of the marine life of the Red Sea would do credit to any marine biologist today, and there are realistic portrayals of the king and queen of Punt, depicted as almost obese compared with the elegantly slender Egyptians. Column capitals are adorned with images of the cow-goddess **Hathor**, depicted with Hatshepsut's features. Other images of the Queen were defaced by her stepson and eventual successor, **Tuthmosis III**, who resented her power and desecrated her temples here and elsewhere, often replacing them with his own.

In later times, the temple became a Coptic Christian monastery, hence its alternative name, **Deir el-Bahari** (Northern Monastery). A crumbling mud-brick gateway to the south of the main road marks the site of the Roman-era settlement.

Temple of Hatshepsut
⏱ daily 08:00–17:30 in winter, 07:00–18:30 in summer
✉ Deir el-Bahari, West Bank, Thebes
💰 E£25

Valley of the Queens
⏱ daily 08:30–16:00 in winter, 07:30–17:00 in summer
✉ West Bank, Thebes
💰 E£25

See Map F–A3 ★★

VALLEY OF THE QUEENS

The canyon-like Valley of the Queens, enclosed by steep cliffs, contains the tombs of more than 70 queens, princes and princesses, the earliest of which date from the late 18th and early 19th Dynasties (ca. 14th to mid-12th century BC). Their burial places are less lavish than the tombs of the pharaohs themselves, but in some ways are even more fascinating. Their decor is less stylized, and their frescoes have a liveliness which is missing from those of the great Pharaonic tombs.

Only a few tombs are open, as archaeological excavation is still in progress in several places, but among those not to be missed are the **Tomb of Nefertari**, favourite wife of Ramses II, and the **Tomb of Amunherkhepshep**, their son. None of Nefertari's treasures escaped the tombraiders, but her tomb is probably the single finest royal tomb in Egypt, comprising three chambers which are adorned from top to bottom with portraits of the queen making offerings to the gods and goddesses. Because of the fragility of these tomb paintings, the tomb has been temporarily closed. Amunherkhepshep died at the age of nine, and within his tomb, vividly coloured murals show the king handing his son over to the guardianship of Anubis, god of the dead (*see* panel, page 31).

> **Nefertari's Tomb**
> Nefertari's Tomb, discovered in 1904, was closed in 1986 for restoration of the finest of all Egyptian tomb paintings. The frescoes, which had been damaged by dehydration and salt crystals, were carefully repaired at a cost of some US$16 million by the Department of Antiquities and the Getty Conservation Organization, and the tomb was reopened to the public in 1997.

Below: *The shattered slopes of the Valley of the Queens hide their secrets well.*

⚙ *See* Map F–A4 | ★★

Temple of Ramses III
⏱ daily 08:30–16:00 in winter, 07:30–17:00 in summer
✉ Medinet Habu, West Bank
💰 E£25

TEMPLE OF RAMSES III

This huge, well-preserved temple was the last great project of the Pharaonic era. The temple was originally surrounded by a large town, known as **Medinet Habu**, which remained an important settlement into the Christian era, but its mud-brick buildings did not weather the centuries as well as the stone temple complex, and almost nothing remains of the town.

Originally surrounded by a ring of ramparts, the entrance to the complex was through a massive gate, the **Migdol**, in which are ceremonial windows where the king could display himself to his people. Three pillared **hypostyle halls** lead to an **inner sanctuary**. The most interesting facet of the building is the outer wall, which is densely engraved with **reliefs** depicting the defeat of the Sea Peoples. Ramses III, who came to the throne in 1195BC, was the first pharaoh of the 20th Dynasty, and is best known for his victories against the invaders from the north, who were probably Achaean Greeks from the coasts and islands of the Aegean Sea, and against the Libyan tribes. The most impressive of the reliefs are on the outer, northern wall of the temple, where a great sea battle is depicted. Within the second inner courtyard there are strikingly colourful and detailed frescoes depicting great religious festivals.

Below: *The walls and columns of the Temple of Medinet Habu are covered with images of the king making offerings to the many gods of Egypt.*

See Map F–B2 ★★

TOMBS OF THE NOBLES

Very few people visit these tombs, yet they are among the most fascinating relics of ancient Egypt. The 'nobles' of the pharaonic era were more akin to a hereditary bureaucratic technocracy than to a feudal, land-owning aristocracy, comprising civil servants, ministers, architects and construction engineers as well as military commanders. Among the first acts of each pharaoh on succeeding to the throne was to begin work on a tomb which would be even more lavish than that of his predecessor, and there is some evidence that higher-ranking members of the noble class may have diverted workers and resources from the grand projects of the pharaohs into completing their own, less dazzling, mausoleums.

Above: *The Tombs of the Nobles are rich in painted scenes of everyday life: here, servants carry funerary furniture and offerings into the tomb of the deceased.*

There are around **400 tombs**, spanning the period from the 6th Dynasty until the Roman era, and around a dozen are well worth a visit. They are divided into five groups, and you need a separate ticket for each group. All are elaborately decorated, and while the huge tombs of the pharaohs are decorated with highly stylized frescoes recounting their achievements and conquests, the smaller tombs of their ministers and advisers are built on a more human scale, and their colourful decorations give the visitor more hints of everyday life in the world of ancient Egypt, with scenes of hunting, sailing and farming.

Tombs of the Nobles
🕐 daily 08:30–16:00 in winter, 07:30–17:00 in summer
✉ Old Qurna, West Bank
💲 E£20 or E£25 for different combinations of two or three tombs

See Map F–A3   ★

Above: *This fresco in the tomb of Sennedjem, in the workmen's village of Deir el-Medina, depicts a number of scenes from life in the ancient world.*

DEIR EL-MEDINA

Southwest of the main complex of the Tombs of the Nobles is believed to have been a **workmen's village**, the home of the artisans and masons who built the tombs of the Valley of the Kings. The skilled craftsmen who lived and worked here were not mere labourers, as their work shows. To mark their own tombs, they built miniature pyramids, around 2m (6ft) high, out of stone and mud brick, and decorated them with motifs imitating those within the tombs of their royal masters.

The remains of over 70 houses, dating from the 18th, 19th and 20th dynasties, can be seen here, on either side of a broad avenue which ran through the centre of the settlement. Deir el-Medina was abandoned around the 13th–12th centuries BC, when Egypt was plunged into Civil War. It takes its modern Arabic name, which means 'monastery of the town', from a later Coptic religious settlement.

Deir el-Medina
🕐 open 08:30–16:00 in winter, 07:30–17:00 in summer
✉ Deir el-Medina, West Bank
💰 E£25

See Map G–B4 ★

MUMMIFICATION MUSEUM

Opened in 1997, this one-room museum is the only museum in the world dedicated to this subject, and casts fascinating light on the religious significance of mummification in ancient Egypt. The collection includes a number of exceptionally well-preserved mummies from ancient Egypt, along with the materials and instruments used to prepare and preserve the body. As well as human mummies, the collection includes animal mummies, among them a baboon, a crocodile and a cat, indicating the religious significance of these creatures in the ancient world. A more recent example is a mummified duck, preserved in 1942 by two archaeologists as part of their research into mummification techniques.

Most of the collection was originally on display in the Egyptian Museum in Cairo, and the centrepiece is a mummy of the high priest Masaharti, which dates from the 21st Dynasty and was discovered at Deir el-Bahri on the West Bank in 1881.

One wall of the museum is hung with panels copied from 13th century BC papyri from the British Museum, illustrating the interesting and elaborate funerary rituals of pharaonic Egypt.

Funerary boats, amulets, and canopic jars are also on display, and a statue of the jackal-headed god Anubis (*see* panel, page 31) stands in the entrance hall of the museum.

Mummification Museum
⏰ 09:00–13:00 daily all year, and 16:00–21:00 in winter, 17:00–22:00 in summer
✉ Sharia Cornish el-Nil, diagonally opposite the Mercure (Etap) Hotel, Luxor
💰 E£40

Below: *Delicately painted on the linen wrappings, the god Osiris protects this mummy of a New Kingdom high priest of Amun on his journey to the Afterlife.*

Above: *Building the Mosque Madrassa of Sultan Hassan, founded in the 14th century, almost bankrupted the sultan. It is even more impressive within than its exterior indicates.*

Cairo's Places of Worship

El-Muayyad Mosque

Named after the sultan who began it in 1415, but also called the Red Mosque, it rises above Bab Zuwayla, and a doorway of black and white marble, framing massive wood and bronze portals, opens into its courtyard.

✉ *Sharia al-Muiz li-Din, Cairo,* ⏰ *09:00–16:00.*

Sultan Hassan Mosque

This very imposing mosque – one of the largest in the world – stands below the medieval citadel, in the centre of Islamic Cairo. Built partly from masonry pillaged from the Great Pyramids of Giza, it was constructed between 1356 and 1363 and is regarded as the most outstanding piece of early Mameluke architecture in Cairo. Four madrassas (Koranic schools) adjoin a huge, spare courtyard, and the towering mausoleum houses not the Mameluke ruler, Sultan Hassan, whose body was never found, but two of his young sons.

✉ *Midan Salah el-Din, Cairo,* ⏰ *09:00–16:00.*

Aq Sunqur Mosque (Blue Mosque)

This mosque was built in 1346, but the blue tiles from which it gets its name were added in the mid-17th century, when the mosque was repaired after being damaged by an earthquake. A stretch of the medieval city wall survives nearby, running northeast from the mosque.

✉ *Sharia Bab el-Wazir, Cairo,* ⏰ *09:00–16:00.*

Mosque of Amr

Cairo's oldest mosque, the Mosque of Amr was built in 642 by Amr Ibn el-As, who led the Arab conquest of Egypt. Partly built into the even more ancient Roman city walls close to the Coptic Museum (see page 25), it contains a stone column which is said to have been miraculously brought from Mecca by Mohammed.

✉ *Sharia Hasan el-Anwar*, **M** *Mari Girgis*, ⊕ *09:00–16:00*.

Sultan Barquq Mosque

Built in the early 15th century and restored in the 1970s, this is the most impressive of numerous mosques which stand among the tombs of sultans and caliphs in medieval Cairo's Northern Cemetery. Its twin minarets and domes are typical of Mameluke religious architecture, and the domes and *minbar* (pulpit) within are beautifully carved and decorated with geometric patterns.

✉ *north of the El-Azhar Mosque and Khan el-Khalili, Cairo*, ⊕ *09:00–16:00*.

Mohammed Ali Mosque

See page 21.

Church of el-Muallaqa (Virgin Mary)

As with most of Cairo's many Coptic churches, many of them founded well over 1000 years ago, this one can be found in the Misr el-Qadima quarter, the centre of Coptic Christianity in Cairo. It was built on the site of the Roman city, on the banks of the Nile. As a minority religion, Coptic Christians have traditionally avoided ostentation, and these churches are usually far more impressive within than their quite plain exteriors suggest. The most accessible, the oldest and the most beautiful is el-Muallaqa. Its fine stonework is

Above and below: *Details from the Mohammed Ali Mosque, begun in 1830 and completed in 1848.*

Below: *Icons of Coptic saints for sale at one of Cairo's churches.*

elaborately carved, and the ivory and cedar altar screens are beautifully worked. The church walls are adorned with lovely icons of the Virgin and the saints.

✉ *near the Mari Girgis metro station, Misr el-Qadima, Cairo,* ⏰ *08:00–16:00.*

Church of Abu Serga (St Sergius)

Very few traces of the original churches remain, but this elegant basilica is typical of the religious architectural style which traces its descent from the Roman basilicas of Alexandria. Beneath it is a crypt which dates from the foundation of this church in the 5th century AD. The original church was destroyed in a fire which swept the city in 750 AD. A wall plaque recalls that the Holy Family are believed to have sheltered here (or in the cave which forms the crypt) after their flight into Egypt.

✉ *off Sharia Mari Girgis, Misr el-Qadima, Cairo,* ⏰ *08:00–16:00.*

Church of Sitt Barbara (St Barbara)

Within this 11th-century church – the largest and among the most impressive of Coptic Cairo's array of churches – is a chapel containing the remains of St Barbara, who was martyred in the 3rd century AD (reputedly by her own father) when she converted to Christianity. Like Abu Serga, the church dates from the 5th century AD, was destroyed in the great fire of AD750 and then rebuilt in the 10th–11th centuries. Its wooden interior is typical of Coptic church architecture. ⊠ *off Sharia Mari Girgis, Misr el-Qadima, Cairo,* ⏱ *08:00–16:00.*

Ben Ezra Synagogue

Only a handful of synagogues remain in Egypt, as the greater part of the country's once numerous Jewish community emigrated to Israel during the 20th century. This is the oldest, and may once have been a church. It is entered via a gateway carved with the six-pointed Star of David. ⊠ *off Sharia Mari Girgis, Misr el-Qadima, Cairo,* ⏱ *08:00–16:00.*

More places of worship can be found on pages 21, 23, 24, 28, 30, 32 and 34.

Cairo's Museums
Museum of Islamic Art

This is not so much a museum of 'fine art' in the Western sense as of craftsmanship and decoration. The museum contains furniture and woodwork, carvings, illuminated books, ceramics and copper and brassware from every era and corner of the Muslim world. ⊠ *corner of Sharia Port Said and Sharia el-Qal'a, Cairo,* ☎ *(02) 390 9930,* ⏱ *temporarily closed for renovation.*

Manyal Palace Museum

Built for King Farouk's uncle in 1903, this Rococo palace is lavishly decorated within and cluttered with ornate furniture, gilt mirrors, heavy drapes, rather gaudy glassware, brass and silverware in profusion. This is indicative of the royal extravagance amid poverty that ultimately led to the overthrow of the Dynasty and the establishment of the Republic. ⊠ *Sharia el-Saray,* ☎ *(02) 368 7495,* ⏱ *daily 08:00–17:00.*

Above: *The Copts (Egyptian Christians) always celebrate Christmas and Easter with age-old ceremony.*

Death on the Nile

Was Tutankhamun really murdered? He was, some writers argue, the puppet of a priesthood keen to reclaim power after being sidelined by his father-in-law and predecessor, Akhenaten. After Tutankhamun's death, the high priest Ay ruled Egypt until his death four years later. But is there any evidence that Ay had the boy king murdered? The latest examination of the mummy in 2005 discounted the theory of a blow to the back of the head and suggested instead that the king may have died from complications following a broken leg.

Above: *Bab Zuwayla is one of the three remaining city gates of Cairo.*

Ra and Other Sun Gods

The ancient Egyptians worshipped the sun in many guises. Ra is pictured as a man with a falcon's head, crowned with the holy disc of the Sun. He crossed the sky in his **solar boat**, rising from the world below in the east and setting in the west, which the Egyptians associated with the land of the dead. Ra had many identities, including Khepri, the sacred scarab which brings the rising sun, and eventually merged with Amun as the most important ancient deity. Aten (Aton) was another aspect of Ra, as was Atum, the setting sun.

Solar Boat Museum

This museum was built of glass to house one of two funeral barques unearthed in good condition from one of the boat pits around the Pyramid in 1954. Such vessels, of unknown significance, were apparently commonly buried in sealed pits within pyramid walls. They may have been used for priestly pilgrimages, or to assist the deceased Pharaoh in his voyage to the afterworld. Visitors are asked to wear special footwear to avoid tracking sand into the museum.
✉ *south of the Great Pyramid of Cheops, Pyramid Road, 18km (11 miles) southwest of central Cairo,* ⏰ *08:00–16:00 daily,* 💰 *E£80.*

Other Places of Interest

Bab Zuwayla

More than 60 towered and vaulted **gates** pierced the city walls which ringed medieval Muslim Cairo. Most have vanished, along with all but a few stretches of the medieval ramparts, which were demolished during the 19th century to allow the growing city to expand beyond its former limits. Only three of the gates still survive, and Bab Zuwayla is one of the most atmospheric. Under the Mamelukes it was a place of execution, and it owes its survival partly to the reputation of a 19th-century saint, **Mitwali**, who is said to have performed several healing miracles here. Local people who hope the saint will still intervene to heal them hang rags of clothing or locks of hair by the gate.
✉ *Sharia al-Muiz li-Din, Cairo,* ⏰ *09:00–18:00* 💰 *E£10.*

Nilometer

The Coptic quarter once stood closer to the main channel of the Nile than it does now, the river having changed course over the centuries. A narrow channel separates Misr el-Qadima from Roda Island, at the tip of which is the 9th-century Nilometer, an eight-sided stone column, marked off in cubits, which was used to measure floods and predict the harvest. It is the only Islamic Nilometer in Egypt (there are several pharaonic ones).

⊠ *Roda Island,* ⊕ *10:00–17:00,* ☗ *E£10.*

Sightseeing in Luxor
Old Qurna Village

The old-fashioned, brightly painted mud-brick houses of Old Qurna village, just west of the main road, are splashes of colour against the barren hillsides. All the villagers have now been relocated to the more modern village at New Qurna, among the fields about 4.5km (2.8 miles) closer to the river, on the El-Fadliya irrigation canal. Some

of their ancestral homes bear cheerful, amateur mural paintings of buses, boats and planes which indicate that their owner made the Muslim pilgrimage to Mecca.

⊠ *West Bank, Luxor.*

Colossi of Memnon

These battered figures radiate an ambience of incredible age which has an undeniable impact. To the right of the main road, opposite the Memnon Hotel, 3km (2 miles) west of the ferry landing, the two colossal, seated statues are all that is left of the vanished **Temple of Amenophis III**. Much damaged (they lack facial features), the colossi

---

Osiris and Isis
Osiris, the lord of the underworld, is depicted both seated and standing. Like Amun, he carries the flail and crook of kingship and his conical crown has ram's horns. Osiris was said to have taught the Egyptians cultivation, and ruled with his bride and sister, **Isis**, who bore him a son, the hawk-headed god **Horus**. Osiris was murdered by his jealous brother Seth, who chopped his body into 14 parts which he threw into the Nile. Isis hunted for each part, and buried each where she found it, which is why there were so many Osiris temples along the Nile.

Below: *The Colossi of Memnon mark the site of a vanished temple.*

Below: *The head of Ramses II at the Ramesseum has suffered at the hands of vandals over the centuries.*

have been a tourist attraction for more than two millennia. In the time of the Ptolemies they were believed by the Greeks to represent a mythical Ethiopian king, **Memnon**, who was killed by Achilles during the Trojan war.
✉ *New Qurna Road, West Bank, Luxor,* ⏱ *all hours.*

Ramesseum

Tumbled columns mark the location of the huge funerary temple of Ramses II, now almost entirely in ruins but still worth visiting to see the toppled colossus of the great pharaoh.
✉ *below Old Qurna village,* 💰 *E£25.*

Temple of Khnum

The Temple of Khnum, the ram-headed god of potters and cataracts, is well worth a visit from Luxor, though the 120km (75-mile) round trip takes approximately one hour each way. The temple stands

close to the river bank, and has not yet been entirely excavated. Its most notable feature is its hypostyle hall, with 24 columns which support a remarkably intact stone slab roof. The temple is, by Egyptian standards, quite recent: it was begun during the 2nd century BC, during the reign of **Ptolemy VI**, an ancestor of Cleopatra, and was still being used for worship 500 years later, during the reign of the Roman emperor **Decius**. The Temple of Khnum can be visited independently by taxi within a police-escorted convoy, or on an escorted tour from your hotel in Luxor, and is also a regular stop on most of the cruise boat itineraries on the journey between Luxor and Aswan.
✉ *Town centre, Esna,* ⏱ *06:00–17:30 in winter, 06:00–18:30 in summer,* 💰 *E£15.*

ACTIVITIES
Sport and Recreation

The top spectator sport in Egypt is **football**, with Cairo club Zamalek and its rival Al-Ahly dominating the league. In a country where ownership of a TV is far from universal, attendance at all games is high, and tickets are hard to come by, but your hotel concierge may be able to find you tickets for a top match. Be prepared, though, to be overwhelmed by the sheer numbers of spectators and their enthusiasm for the game.

In winter, Cairo and Luxor have a perfect climate for **golf** and **tennis**. Most large hotels have tennis courts (often floodlit for night use in summer) and several hotels around Cairo also have golf courses. Among the newest is the **Dreamland Golf and Tennis Resort**, with a new nine-hole championship golf course and golf academy, tennis academy, and on-site Hilton Hotel. Other courses include **El-Gezira Sporting Club**, with an 18-hole course. Golf holidays can also be organized by **NTC Golf Travel**.

The British left Cairo's upper crust with a taste for rowing on the river, Oxford and Cambridge style, and experienced oarspeople can join an eight (crew) at **Al-Nil Sporting Club**. Friday is the busiest day, with frequent inter-club competitions between Cairo rowing clubs.

Almost all the higher category (four-star and up) hotels have swimming pools, and if you are staying in more modest accommodation you can usually gain access to one of these by paying a daily fee.

Above: *Balloon flights over the Valley of the Kings, Karnak and Luxor offer a unique view.*

Dreamland Golf and Tennis Resort
⊠ 6th October City Road, Cairo ☍ dream golf@ie-eg.com
🖳 www. dreamlandgolf.com

El-Gezira Sporting Club
⊠ El-Zamalek, Cairo
☎ (02) 736 0434

NTC Golf Travel
⊠ 16 Geziret el-Arab Street, Mohandeseen, Cairo ☎ (02) 346 0466
📞 (02) 302 7016
🖳 www. ntcgolftravel.com

Al-Nil Sporting Club
⊠ Sharia Cornish el-Nil
☎ (02) 393 4350

Above: *Camels are more often used to carry tourists than to transport cargo.*

Camel and Horseback Rides

The first of the crowd of peddlers, baksheesh-seekers and touts who are bound to assail you on your arrival at Giza will probably be the camel-drivers, determined to sell you a cruise on the 'ship of the desert'.

Although a camel ride around the pyramids must be one of the greatest Egyptian tourism cliches, it is also one of those 'must do' experiences – if only because giving in to their blandishments is the only known way of dealing with these extremely persistent hustlers. Most camel rides take less than an hour and are a far from comfortable experience. Horses and guides can also be hired at Giza for a three-hour desert ride to Saqqara, but this is for experienced riders only.

Cycling

The bicycle is a popular means of transport in **Cairo**, but only the very bravest visitor will feel like challenging Cairo's killer traffic, heat and air pollution on a bike. Cycling around **Luxor** (where there is little traffic and the countryside is mostly flat) is a much more attractive proposition, allowing you to visit outlying villages along the Nile and also to visit Karnak and the West Bank sites at your own pace. Bikes can be hired at all Luxor hotels and from many shops and travel agencies around town, costing from E£10–E£20 daily.

Balloons Over Egypt
✉ PO Box 52, Sharia Khaled Ibn el-Walid, Luxor
☎ (095) 237 6515
📠 (095) 237 0638

Soliman Hot Air Balloons, Luxor
☎ and 📠 (095) 237 0116

Hot-air Ballooning

Drifting over the hills of the West Bank, the Valley of the Kings, the Nile and the rooftops of Luxor in a hot-air balloon is wonderful – the experience of a lifetime. Balloon companies include **Balloons Over Egypt**, with desks in the lobbies of the Hilton, Sheraton and Ibis hotels, and **Soliman Hot Air Balloons**.

Felucca Sailing

The shallow-bottomed, lateen-rigged sailing boats known as feluccas, with their triangular white sails, are a common sight on the Nile – in fact, they are almost as well known a symbol of Egypt as the pyramids. They are still used to carry produce and passengers on short journeys up, down and across the river, but are more commonly on hire by the day or half day to visitors. In **Cairo**, feluccas can be hired from landing stages on the Corniche waterfront in front of the Semiramis Hotel, or opposite the Hotel Meridien, for around E£20–E£30 per hour (depending on how well you bargain). At **Luxor**, the felucca owners tout for passengers along the Cornish el-Nil and a popular destination is 'Banana Island', some 5km (3 miles) downriver from the city. If you have time for only one felucca trip, do choose Luxor, where the palm-lined banks of the Nile, islands, and desert hills of the West Bank are a much more peaceful and attractive setting than the cityscape of Cairo.

> **Feluccas**
> The gaff-rigged (or lateen-rigged) sail that propels the Nile feluccas is the same triangular sail that carried Arab trade from the Red Sea to the East Indies – and is still used on trading dhows throughout the Arab world. On the Nile, most trade now goes by motor barge. In the 19th century, western visitors chartering a wooden felucca insisted that the boat was submerged for several days to kill off fleas and bedbugs lurking in the cracks of the wooden hull, but nowadays vermin are less of a problem.

Below: *Feluccas with their triangular sails are a common sight on the Nile.*

Fun for Children

Cairo and Luxor are not ideal destinations for families with small children, as there are few purpose-built attractions and activities for little ones. That said, major hotels in both cities have pools and gardens which will keep smaller children happy, and older children and teenagers will enjoy camel rides at the pyramids, and felucca sailing on the Nile at Luxor (see pages 46–47).

Organized Tours
Cairo

Numerous organized tours of Cairo are available from every hotel and through the tourist offices, and for many people visiting the top attractions, a tour led by an expert guide is a more attractive option than trying to understand these ancient sites alone. Individual visitors inevitably draw swarms of amateur and not very reliable guides as well as touts and peddlers. There are a number of **language** options, with English, French, Italian and German (and, of course, Arabic) the most easily available.

Tours range from **city tours** and **guided museum visits** to half-day or full-day visits to the attractions close to **Cairo**. There are also **excursions** away from the city, for example to the Western Desert, the Mediterranean Coast, the Red Sea and trips by air to Luxor, Aswan and Abu Simbel (see Excursions, pages 78–83).

The most popular half-day tour takes visitors to the **Sphinx**, the **Great Pyramids of Giza** (usually including a guided visit to the tomb chamber of the Pyramid of Cheops), and the **Solar Boat Museum**, next to the Pyramid of Cheops. Another half-day itinerary includes visits to the pyramids of **Saqqara** and the open-air museum and mummification beds at **Memphis**. There are also half-day and full-day **city tours** which include guided visits to the Egyptian Antiquities Museum, Khan el-Khalili bazaar area, the Citadel of Saladin and the Coptic quarter. Almost all tours include several stops for **shopping**, generally at shops with which the guide or tour company has a discreet commission agreement. This can be irritating if you are more interested in Egypt's ancient heritage than in its souvenir stores.

Tours of **Cairo by night** are also available, including the spectacular Sound and Light Show at the Pyramids of Giza, or an evening of entertainment with belly-dancing at one of the many restaurant-nightclubs in Giza suburb.

Other popular excursions include full-day or half-day **cruises on the Nile**.

Misr Travel, the official Egyptian Tourist Authority tour company, arranges all these and more and can also arrange tailor-made guided tours for individuals. Other travel agents offering a full range of group tours as well as individual arrangements include **American Express** and **Thomas Cook**.

Above: *The Khan el-Khalili bazaar in the heart of medieval Cairo is a shopper's paradise – but be prepared to haggle.*
Opposite: *A variety of full- or half-day Nile cruises are available from Cairo.*

Misr Travel (Cairo)
☎ (02) 682 7029
📠 (02) 683 4216

Misr Travel (Luxor)
✉ next to the Winter Palace Hotel, Luxor
☎ (095) 238 0951

American Express
☎ (02) 574 7991

Thomas Cook
☎ (02) 2696 5172

Luxor

Tight security at the key Luxor sites, including Karnak and the Temple of Luxor, means it is easier to explore these without being hassled by crowds of would-be guides. However, as is the case in Cairo, a tour led by an expert guide can enhance your understanding of these ancient places, and there is a wide choice of organized itineraries available – these can be booked at all major hotels (even if you are not staying at one of these) and at travel agencies including the local branch of **Misr Travel** (*see* panel, page 49).

Luxor's vast array of sights demands several days to explore. Available tours include half-day or one-day tours of the **West Bank** sites usually combining the Valley of the Kings (with a mandatory visit to Tutankhamun's Tomb) with the Valley of the Queens, the Temple of Hatshepsut, and sometimes the Tombs of the Nobles and the Workmen's Village. Taking two or even three half-day tours is preferable to trying to cram all these into one day. On the **East Bank**, most tours combine the Karnak complex and the Temple of Luxor in a half-day or one-day itinerary including a break for lunch. As in Cairo, almost all tours include more than a few stops for **shopping**. Luxor has little to offer by **night**, but organized tours combining a visit to the Sound and Light Spectacular at Karnak, followed by an evening of music and belly dancing – usually in a hotel restaurant – are also on offer.

Photography

Take plenty of film. Egyptian shops offer only a limited range of standard print film, which may have been stored in less than perfect conditions. Slide film is hard to find. Processing in Egypt is not always reliable. For best results, take pictures first thing in the morning or late afternoon – the fierce midday sun makes photography difficult. Using a flash is banned in most tombs and museums. Some attendants may offer to turn a blind eye for baksheesh, but you should resist the temptation as intense light damages ancient frescoes.

Half-day, full-day and evening **Nile cruises** are also available. If staying in one of Luxor's budget hotels you are likely to be offered a **donkey tour** of the West Bank. Be warned that this must be the least comfortable way of seeing the sights – it is by far preferable to rent a bicycle and be your own guide.

Misr Travel also organizes full-day tours to the temple sites at **Dendera** (64km/40 miles north of Luxor), the most impressive complex of temples between Cairo and Luxor, and **Abydos** (100km/60 miles northwest of Luxor) with its superb Mortuary Temple of Seti I. Due to the security situation, it may be permitted to visit these sites only as part of an organized group tour.

South of Luxor, full-day tours combine visits to the Temple of Khnum at Esna (60 km/38 miles from Luxor) and the Temple of Horus at Edfu (115km/70 miles from Luxor).

Alternative Cairo

Cairo is a socially and politically conservative society, as seen by the many young women adopting the traditional *hejab* (head covering), and has not been fertile ground for the development of an openly gay, still less lesbian, alternative scene. Homosexuality is not illegal, but controversial prosecutions are sometimes made under the prostitution laws. The scene is discreet to the point of being secretive, and there are no 'out' gay venues, though the Taverne bar at the Nile Hilton has a reputation as a rendezvous for gay men.

> **Baksheesh**
> Wherever you go in Egypt you will meet requests, even demands, for baksheesh (a tip) from anyone who does you any kind of service – or indeed none at all. It's up to you how much you choose to give, but it's a good idea to keep a stash of small change and small bills. Even if you agree a fixed price for a camel ride or felucca cruise before setting out, your guide or boatman is bound to demand a healthy kickback on top of that.

Opposite: *The entrance to one of the many tombs in the Valley of the Kings, Luxor.*
Below: *A dramatic sunset on the Nile at Luxor.*

Above: *Shops and market stalls spill over into busy urban streets.*

Shops and Malls – Cairo

Museum Shop, Egyptian Antiquities Museum

In the nation's most important museum, this shop sells officially approved, high-quality reproductions of scarabs, seals, papyrus, tomb paintings, busts and statues of gods, queens and pharaohs, and copies of jewellery worn in ancient times, and is probably the best place to buy your souvenirs of ancient Egypt. Prices are fixed.
⊠ *Midan el-Tahrir*, **M** *Midan el-Tahrir*, ☎ *(02) 575 4319*, ☾ *09:00–18:30 daily.*

Egyptian Crafts Centre/Fair Trade Egypt

Good choice of traditional crafts, including camel-hair and wool rugs and blankets, cottons from Upper Egypt, beads and papyrus paintings. Prices are more or less fixed, and profits help rural development and village communities.
⊠ *27 Yehia Ibrahim, El-Zamalek*, ☎ *(02) 735 1045*, **M** *Zamalek (when complete)*, ☾ *09:00–20:00 Sat–Thu, 09:00–18:00 Fri.*

The National Mashrabiyyah Institute

The National Mashrabiyyah Institute (also known as NADIM) sells the finest examples of these traditionally carved wooden lattice screens and is one of the few places where they are still made by skilled craftsmen. Prices are high, but these are superb collectors' items.
⊠ *Abu Rawash Industrial Zone, off Cairo–Alexandria*

Desert Road,
☎ *(02) 539 1601,*
📠 *(02) 539 1609,*
M *Dokki,* ⊕ *09:00–13:00 except Fri.*

Arkadia Mall

One of Cairo's largest shopping malls, part of the Conrad International Hotel complex, has around 500 shops and boutiques, with major international brands strongly represented, and numerous smart outlets where Cairenes buy their fashion clothes, shoes, sportswear, jewellery and accessories. There is also a food court selling everything from burgers to *fuul* and kebabs.

✉ *Sharia Corniche el-Nil, Bulaq,* **M** *Bulaq,* ⊕ *09:00–20:00 Sun–Thu, 09:00–11.00 and 13:00–20:00 Fri, closed Sat.*

First Residence Mall

Cairo's most exclusive and expensive shopping mall is part of a posh apartment complex in the suburb of Giza. Full of the world's most costly brand name boutiques, this is where the city's rich spend their shopping time in air-conditioned comfort. There is little here that you would not find in any major city worldwide, but it's worth a visit if only for the huge contrast with the street-level shopping of Cairo's bazaar areas.

✉ *35 Sharia el-Giza,* **M** *Giza,* ⊕ *09:00–20:00 Sun–Thu, 09:00–11.00 and 13:00–20:00 Fri, closed Sat.*

Nagada

This shop sells fine cottons from Upper Egypt, cotton and woollen traditional clothes, earthenware pottery from the Nile Valley, beads and other jewellery, and brass and pottery lamps.

✉ *13 Refa'a Street, Dokki,* ☎ *(02) 748*

Haggling

Even in more sophisticated stores, a certain amount of bargaining may gain you a discount of anything up to 20 per cent off the asking price. In markets, start by offering about a quarter of the asking price and settle for anything from one third to two thirds: generally, anything over half what the merchant first asks for is generous, and if you can settle for around one third you are getting the best of the deal.

Best Buys

- Antique brassware
- Alabaster work
- Muski glassware and ceramics
- Rugs and textiles, especially cotton
- Essential oils from the Perfume Bazaar
- Herbs and spices
- Handmade *gallabiya* robes
- Museum-certified reproductions of archaeological finds from museum shops
- Hand-painted papyrus

6663, 🖳 *www.
nagada.net*
🕑 *09:30–17:00 daily.*

Markets
Khan el-Khalili

The Khan el-Khalili
bazaar area has fan-
tastic bargains for
those prepared to
bargain hard, but
remember that hag-
gling is not only a
way of life but a
form of entertain-
ment – don't make a
battle out of it, just
move on to another
stall if you can't
make a deal. As in
medieval times,
traders in the same
commodity or craft
tend to be grouped
together, which
makes it easier to
compare prices. Visit
the **Perfume Bazaar**
area for sweet-
smelling essential
oils, exported world-
wide to leading per-
fumiers. An-Nahassin,
the Street of the
Coppersmiths, is
where to find
engraved brass trays
and tabletops, coffee-
pots, water pitchers
and cups. Other good
buys include fine
Egyptian cotton and
silk, typical Egyptian
clothing for men and
women such as the
long *gallabiya* robes
worn by both sexes,
perfumed oils, and
spices – you will find
these piled in colour-
ful heaps beside the
brass scales and
weights in spice mer-
chants' stores. You
will also find rows of
shops selling
nargilehs (water
pipes) in the Souq el-
Nahaseen part of the
bazaar, which is also
a good place to find
fancy backgammon
boards inlaid with
polished bone and
hardwood patterns
(*see also* page 22).
🕑 *around
10:00–20:00 Mon–Sat,
closed Sun.*

Souq el-Sagha
(Goldsmith's Bazaar)

There are goldsmiths
and silversmiths all
over the medieval
quarter, but the best
are here, as they have
been for centuries,
on Sharia al-Muiz li-
Din Allah. Styles tend
towards the ostenta-
tiously garish, and as
everywhere in the
Middle East price is
determined more by
weight than by
craftsmanship.
✉ *Sharia al-Muiz li-
Din Allah,* 🕑 *around
10:00–20:00 Mon–Sat,
closed Sun.*

Sharia el-Khayamiyya
(Street of the Tentmakers)

Among the last of
Cairo's old covered
markets, this street is
packed with work-
shops which no
longer specialize in
tent making for
camel caravans, but
instead excel in mak-
ing patchwork cush-
ions, throws and wall
hangings decorated
with various village
scenes, geometric
patterns or Koranic
scripts.
✉ *Sharia el-Khaya-
miyya,* 🕑 *around
10:00–20:00 Mon–Sat,
closed Sun.*

Kerdassa Village

This tourist shopping village east of Giza's pyramids is a very good spot to search out rugs and carpets made by Egypt's Bedouin nomads, leather goods such as cushions and saddlebags, cotton textiles and *gallabiyas*.

✉ *Sharia Maryutiya, Giza,* **M** *Giza,* ⏱ *around 10:00–20:00 Mon–Sat, closed Sun.*

Shopping in Luxor

Luxor's opportunities for shopping are more limited than in Cairo.

Tourist Bazaar

Close to the Temple of Luxor, this covered market area is packed with stalls and open-fronted shops selling leather goods, cotton clothing, sandals, and *gallabiyas*. Several merchants also sell copies of finds from ancient tombs (quality varies widely so shop around) and colourful

paintings on papyrus.
✉ *Sharia el-Karnak, Luxor.*

Old Qurna Alabaster Workshops

In the village of Old Qurna, many villagers have taken to producing a range of handmade products carved or lathe-turned from local **alabaster**, a creamy-coloured, translucent stone. Bowls, vases, goblets, candlesticks and ashtrays are on offer. Haggling over the price is the order of the day here.
✉ *Old Qurna village.*

Above: *Ancient skills are still used by tentmakers and mousetrap vendors in Egyptian bazaars.*

Muski Glass

Old fashioned, hand-blown translucent muski glass is a speciality of the Khan el-Khalili, and with some haggling you can find attractive glasses, bowls and jugs at good prices. Most muski glassware is turquoise-green in colour, but red glass can also be found.

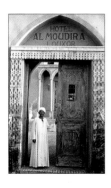

Above: *Al Moudira Hotel, a boutique hotel on the West Bank of Luxor*

WHERE TO STAY

As you would expect from such a vast city, **Cairo** has a huge range of accommodation options, ranging from palatial, brand new properties operated by major international chains, with luxury facilities fit for a pharaoh, to down and dirty budget properties. The good news is that mid-range and even luxury properties are competitively priced, and there is really no need to seek out the cheapest budget properties when you can stay in considerable comfort for remarkably little. **Luxor** has a rather wider range of clean and comfortable budget accommodation, but here too mid-range and luxury hotels can often offer real bargain prices.

Hotels are rated from one to five stars, but visitors are advised to avoid those rated less than three stars. For much of the year, facilities such as air conditioning and a pool are necessities, not luxuries, and budget hotels are likely to lack even such basic amenities as hot water, mosquito nets or clean sheets.

In Cairo, most tourist-standard and luxury hotels are in the Garden City and Zamalek areas on the banks of the Nile, out of town in the posh business and residential suburb of Heliopolis (which is conveniently close to the airport) and in the Giza area, where you will pay extra for a room with a view of the pyramids. Decent budget properties can be found in central Cairo, and in the Zamalek district (the northern half of Gezira Island), but there are no budget hotels worth recommending in Giza or Heliopolis.

Lists of government-classified hotels in Cairo and Luxor are available from Egyptian Tourist Authority offices overseas and local tourist offices (*see* Travel Tips, page 84).

New Hotels

Cairo is in the throes of a hotel building boom, with many new mega-luxury resort hotels, including the Movenpick Hotel, Media City, Giza, with three restaurants, three pools and its own leisure centre; the ultra-fabulous Four Seasons Cairo at Nile Plaza, with four restaurants, a business centre and health club in the Garden City area; Heliopolis Inter-Continental, a luxury complex with 717 rooms, including 73 self-contained bungalows and chalets, part of a \$600 million shopping, office, and entertainment complex called City Stars.

Central Cairo

• LUXURY

Four Seasons

(Map A–C4)

Top-notch luxury and superb dining in this new chain hotel, close to the heart of Cairo.

✉ *1089 Cornish, Garden City,* ☎ *(02) 791 7000,* ℡ *(02) 791 6900,* 🖥 *www. fourseasons.com*

Cairo Marriott Hotel (Map A–B2)

Palatial hotel on the banks of the Nile, in lush gardens, with 1250 rooms and suites, 15 bars and restaurants, and a huge pool.

✉ *Sharia el-Gezira, El-Zamalek,* ☎ *(02) 728 3000,* ℡ *(02) 735 8240,* 🖥 *www. cairomarriott.com*

Grand Hyatt

(Map A–C4)

Modern hotel with all the facilities you would expect from this prestigious international hotel chain. All rooms have Nile views. Superb revolv-ing restaurant on the 40th floor.

✉ *Sharia Cornish el-Nil, Roda,* ☎ *(02) 362 1717,* ℡ *(02) 362 1927.*

Semiramis Inter-Continental Cairo

(Map A–C3)

Luxury chain hotel with superb views of the Nile and the city, combined with central location, close to the Egyptian Antiquities Museum and down-town shopping.

✉ *Sharia Cornish el-Nil, Roda,* ☎ *(02) 795 7171,* ℡ *(02) 796 3020.*

• MID-RANGE

Atlas Zamalek Hotel (Map A–A2)

Among the more com-fortable of Cairo's mid-range hotels, this four-star is a little way from the city centre. Facilities include rooftop pool, sauna, solarium, gym, chil-dren's pool, bar and restaurant.

✉ *20 Sharia Gameat el Dowal el Arabia, Mohandiseen,* ☎ *(02) 346 6569,* ℡ *(02) 347 6958.*

Europa Cairo Hotel

(Map K–A2)

A rooftop pool, shops, choice of restaurants and a location not far from the sights make this hotel worth re-commending. It also has a nightclub and bar, which means it can be noisy at times.

✉ *300 Pyramids Road, Dokki,* ☎ *(02) 581 5940,* ℡ *(02) 584 9130,* 🖥 *www.hotelsegypt. com/cairo/europa_cairo*

• BUDGET

Longchamps Hotel

(Map A–B1)

Three-star, family-run hotel on 5th and 6th floors of an apartment building, good value for money. There's a bar on the roof terrace, most rooms have a balcony or terrace, and continental break-fast is included in the price. Airport transfers also available. Rooms have en-suite shower, air conditioning.

✉ *21 Sharia Ismail Mohammed, El-Zamalek,* ☎ *(02) 735 2311,* ℡ *(02) 735 9644,* ✆ *hotel.longchamps@*

web.de ⌨ www.
hotellongchamps.com

Cosmopolitan Hotel (Map A–D3)

This charming old Art Deco hotel has antique furniture and decor, but also modern comforts including air conditioning.
✉ 1 Sharia Ibn Tahlab, Qasr el-Nil, Cairo, ☎ (02) 392 3663, ☏ (02) 393 3531.

El-Hussein Hotel

(Map A–F3)
In the heart of Islamic Cairo, this small hotel is graded two-star, but has better facilities and standards than this suggests, including rooms with *ensuite* bathroom and a roof terrace overlooking the bazaar area.
✉ Midan Hussein, Sharia el-Azhar, Cairo, ☎ (02) 591 8664, ☏ (02) 591 8089.

Flamenco Hotel

(Map A–B1)
Comfortable, modern, and well managed three-star. Some rooms have Nile views.

✉ 2 Geziret el-Wusta, El-Zamalek, ☎ (02) 735 0815, ☏ (02) 735 0819, ☍ sales@ flamencohotels.com

Windsor Hotel

(Map A–D2)
Its faded grandeur recalls the decades (before independence) when it was a British Officers' Club. Huge choice of rooms and a great atmosphere.
✉ 19 Sharia Alfy, ☎ (02) 591 5277, ☏ (02) 592 1621, ☍ wdoss@link.net

Heliopolis

• *LUXURY*

Concorde el-Salam Hotel (Map K–C1)

This 320-room hotel stands amid manicured lawns and palm trees. Its 37 business rooms have two-line phones, voicemail and dataports. Facilities include a cinema, casino, summer terrace for dining, dancing and live entertainment, squash, riding and bridge club.
✉ 65 Sharia Abdel Hamid Badawi, Heliopolis, ☎ (02) 622

4000, ☏ (02) 622 6037, ⌨ www.
concorde-hotels.com

JW Marriott Hotel Mirage City

(Map K–C1)
Recently opened, it has an 18-hole golf course, sports club, health spa and water park.
✉ Ring Road, Mirage City, Cairo, ☎ (02) 411 5588, ☏ (02) 411 2266, ⌨ marriott.com/hotels

Le Meridien Heliopolis (Map K–B1)

In landscaped gardens, this hotel is near the Presidential Palace and International Conference Centre.
✉ 51 El-Orouba Street, Heliopolis, ☎ (02) 290 5055, ☏ (02) 291 8591, ☍ reservations@ meridien-heliopolis.com
⌨ www.lemeridien-heliopolis.com

• *MID-RANGE*

Baron Hotel

(Map K–B1)
A budget property only by Heliopolis standards, ten minutes' drive from the airport, 126 four-star

rooms, four restaurants, five minutes' walk from Heliopolis's shopping and restaurant streets.
⊠ PO Box 2351, Horreya, 11362 Heliopolis, ☎ (02) 291 2468, 📠 (02) 290 7077.

Giza
• *LUXURY*
Four Seasons
(Map A–B4)
One of the best hotels in Cairo, intoxicating levels of service, superb facilities, and a wealthy clientele. It is within the First Residence residential complex, Cairo's address to impress.
⊠ 35 Sharia el-Giza, Giza, ☎ (02) 573 1212, 📠 (02) 568 1616, 💻 www.fourseasons.com

Cataract Pyramids Resort (Map J–D1)
With nine bars and restaurants, this five-star combines the attractions of the city with the pleasures of a holiday resort hotel. Near the pyramids of Saqqara and Giza and

40 minutes by freeway from the airport.
⊠ Saqqara Road, El-Haraneya, Giza, ☎ (02) 384 2901, 📠 (02) 384 2902.

Sheraton Royal Gardens Hotel
(Map J–D1)
Super-luxury five-star, two superb pools, palm gardens, Japanese, Mexican and Lebanese restaurants, shopping arcade, nightclub and bar, limousine service and much more.
⊠ Sharia Helmeiat el-Ahram, Giza, ☎ (02) 781 2211, 📠 (02) 781 1441.

Mena House Oberoi (Map B)
Superb hotel near the pyramids, with everything going for it, but perhaps trades a bit much on its reputation.
⊠ Sharia el-Ahram, Giza, ☎ (02) 377 3222, 📠 (02) 376 7777.

Le Meridien Pyramids (Map J–D1)
Fine resort-style hotel

with unrivalled views of the Great Pyramids from its palm gardens and pools. Restaurants serve Mediterranean, oriental and Mexican cuisine among others.
⊠ Midan el-Remaya, Giza, ☎ (02) 383 0383, 📠 (02) 383 1730, ✆ c.s@meridien-pyramids.com.eg
💻 www.lemeridien-pyramids.com

Maadi
• *MID-RANGE*
CairoTel (Map J–D1)
With views of the Giza and Saqqara pyramids, this comfortable four-star has a pool, gardens, and four restaurants and café-bars.
⊠ Maadi Entrance, Maadi, Cairo, ☎ and 📠 (02) 358 6787, ✆ cairotel@maadi.com

Luxor (East Bank)
• *LUXURY*
Sofitel Winter Palace Hotel
(Map G–A4)
The oldest, grandest hotel in Luxor. Built in 1897 and recently restored (by French

hotel chain Sofitel) to its former glory, with cream-coloured stucco, high-ceiling public rooms, uniformed waiters, pool, tennis court and views over the Nile.

✉ *Sharia Cornish el-Nil, Luxor,* ☎ *(095) 238 0422,* 📠 *(095) 237 4087.*

Sheraton Luxor Resort (Map G–A6)

Palatial hotel on the banks of the Nile with 290 rooms and suites, including 90 'chalet rooms' in private villas. Four restaurants, two bars (one of them by the pool), a disco, and floodlit tennis courts.

✉ *Sharia Khaled Ibn el-Walid, Luxor,* ☎ *(095) 237 4957,* 📠 *(095) 237 4941,* 🖥 *reservation_luxor_egypt@sheraton.com*

Hilton International Luxor

(Map G–C1)

Only 500m from the Karnak temple complex, this is the most luxurious of Luxor's international chain hotels. Lovely gardens beside the Nile, an outdoor pool, and a choice of restaurants.

✉ *Sharia Cornish el-Nil, El-Karnak,* ☎ *(095) 237 4933,* 📠 *(095) 237 6571.*

Nile Palace

(Map G–B4)

Large resort-style hotel with 304 rooms (most facing the Nile) and its own shopping arcade, pool, fitness centre, restaurants including a French-style café-bar.

✉ *Sharia Cornish el-Nil, Luxor,* ☎ *(095) 236 6999,* 📠 *(095) 236 5666,*

Jolie Ville Movenpick Luxor Resort (Map G–A6)

On a tropical island, this resort complex has six bars and restaurants, four tennis courts, a pool, and 332 bungalow-style rooms and suites, each with its own terrace.

✉ *Crocodile Island, Luxor,* ☎ *(095) 237 4855,* 📠 *(095) 237 4936,* 🖥 *resort.luxor@movenpick.com*

• MID-RANGE
Mercure Inn Luxor

(Map G–B4)

This comfortable four-star is near the Temple of Luxor, has five restaurants (including poolside Italian), and rooms with balconies.

✉ *10 Temple Street, Luxor,* ☎ *(095) 238 0721,* 📠 *(095) 238 0051.*

Gaddis Hotel

(Map G–A6)

Small recently renovated four-star with *en-suite* bathrooms, air conditioning, minibar, satellite TV and video, views of the Nile or the pool and gardens. Two restaurants and a quirky pub, competitive rates.

✉ *Sharia Khaled Ibn el-Walid, Luxor,* ☎ *(095) 238 2838,* 📠 *(095) 238 2837.*

• BUDGET
St Joseph Hotel

(Map G–A6)

Good value three-

star, 75 air-conditioned rooms with *en-suite* shower, rooftop pool, bar, restaurant, garden terrace. Many rooms have Nile views.
✉ *Sharia Khaled Ibn el-Walid, Luxor,* ☎ *(095) 238 1707,* ✆ *(095) 238 7727.*

Shady Hotel

(Map G–B5) Centrally located three-star with pool and garden. All 50 rooms have *en-suite* bathrooms and air conditioning. Poolside coffee shop-restaurant open round the clock.
✉ *Television Street, Luxor,* ☎ *(095) 238 1262,* ✆ *(095) 237 4859.*

Karnak Hotel

(Map J–E4) Opposite the Hilton and near the Karnak complex, this hotel has a pool, a tidy garden area and a great location.
✉ *Sharia Cornish el-Nil, Karnak,* ☎ *and* ✆ *(095) 237 4155.*

Luxor (West Bank)

• LUXURY

Al Moudira Hotel

(Map G–A3) 54-room boutique hotel in gardens, near Medinet Habu and the Nile. It also has a pool, air-conditioned rooms, *en-suite* bathrooms.
✉ *West Bank, Luxor,* ☎ *(012) 392 8332,* ✆ *(012) 322 0528,* ✎ *moudirahotel @yahoo.com* 🖥 *www.moudira.com*

• MID-RANGE/ BUDGET

Pharaohs Hotel

(Map F–B4) Comfortable, near the Temple of Ramses III and convenient for exploring the West Bank independently (it rents bicycles). The only good-value option for those on a less generous budget. Air-conditioned rooms have *en-suite* bathrooms and private terraces, and there is a large swimming pool.
✉ *New Karnak, Luxor,* ☎ *and* ✆ *(095) 231 0702.*

Accommodation in Luxor

Luxor has fewer top-grade luxury properties than Cairo, but does have a solid portfolio of mid-range, value-for-money hotels catering mainly for package holiday-makers, with a sprinkling of comfortable, value-for-money budget properties. Mid-range and luxury hotels are found along Sharia Cornish el-Nil, with views across the river to the West Bank, while budget properties tend to be further from the river. There are one or two luxury and mid-range hotels on the West Bank, but there are no recommendable budget hotels on this side of the river.

Egyptian Restaurants
If there seems to be a dearth of good restaurants outside the walls of Cairo's luxury hotels, put it down to the Egyptian preference for eating at home, *en famille*, rather than going out to dine, even (in fact especially) on special occasions. And if the restaurant you patronize seems deserted, it's probably because you have turned up too early – Egyptians do not sit down to dinner until at least 21:00, often much later.

EATING OUT
What to Eat

Egyptian food is influenced by cultures from all over the Middle East, the Mediterranean and – judging by the huge number of pizzerias, McDonalds, and Kentucky Fried Chicken outlets on Cairo's streets – America too.

Beans and **pulses** figure large on the everyday menu. The staple, national dish is *fuul*, a rich and tasty blend of fava beans spiced up with sesame oil, pepper, salt and lemon and eaten with salad and bread. Another favourite filling meal is *kushari*, a stew of rice, lentils and noodles topped with spicy tomato sauce. Egyptians are fond of flavoursome vegetable dips, too, such as **tahina**, made from sesame seeds, and *baba ghanoug*, made from eggplant, so vegetarians have a range of options.

For ordinary Egyptians in the villages and in the cities, **meat** is a special treat, not something to be eaten every day. Most people breakfast on beans, eggs and cheese and eat lunch, the main meal of the day, in the mid- to late afternoon. Lamb, mutton, chicken and – typically Egyptian – pigeon are among the most prominent items on feast-day or celebratory menus. Pork is, of course, off-limits to Muslims and is rarely seen, even on the menus of international hotels, and beef or steak are rarely found except in the more expensive interna-

tional restaurants. **Seafood** is also hard to find, except in the top Cairo hotel restaurants, although Nile perch (**tilapia**) appears on the menu frequently in tourist hotels.

Most restaurants serve lunch from around 13:00 until as late as 17:00 and dinner from around 19:00, and many of the larger hotels have 24-hour coffee shops serving drinks and snacks around the clock.

Snacks

Everyday snacks sold from stalls and small restaurants all over Cairo and Luxor include *taamiya*. These tasty nuggets of deep-fried mashed white beans, flavoured with herbs and spices, are a favourite nibble and are similar to the felafel of other parts of the Middle East, where they are made from mashed chick peas. Cheap and nutritious, they are a boon to the budget traveller – and indeed to anyone looking for a quick and filling meal. Skewered and grilled meat snacks – invariably mutton – include **kofta** (minced lamb or mutton), **kebab** (chunks of lamb) and *shawarma* (slices of lamb).

Above: *The Nile is a rich source of fish for restaurants.*
Opposite: *In Cairo's traffic, an old-fashioned bicycle is often the fastest way of delivering fresh-baked bread to homes, restaurants and hotels.*

Meze
You will find meze on the menu in many of Cairo's restaurants, especially those patronized by visitors from neighbouring nations. It's a truly transnational display of dishes – dips like hummus and tahina, stuffed vine or cabbage leaves, and lots more. A relic of the Ottoman empire, meze in one form or another is found across the Arab world, as well as in Turkey and Greece.

Above: *This man is making* taamiya – *the cheap, tasty and nutritious staple snack of Egyptian streets.*

Desserts

Egyptian desserts are invariably sticky and sweet, often featuring layers of honey, phyllo pastry and various nuts, cinnamon and other spices. The most common dessert is **baklava**, served in small slices. Similar flavourings are used to make *kunafa*, with a base consisting of fine noodles instead of flat pastry. Cold puddings such as *mahal-labiya* (blancmange) and *ruzz billaban* (rice pudding) are other popular items on the dessert menu.

What to Drink

Islam frowns on alcohol, but that has not stopped the Egyptians developing a not very extensive range of domestic wines, beers and liquors. A recent development has been the importation of French wine-making expertise to relaunch three local **wines** – red, white and rosé – which were previously made from Egyptian-grown grapes by a state-owned monopoly and were almost undrinkable. The white *Cru des Ptolemees*, the rosé *Rubis d'Egypte* and the red *Omar Khayyam* are now quite palatable, though they have some way to go before they can rival the better imported wines which are served in luxury hotels and restaurants.

WHERE TO EAT

A number of local beers are now available, including Egypt's famed **Stella** lager and the darker, tastier **Stella Premium**, as well as the popular **Sakkara Gold**. These are all reliable and well worth a try, though many beer drinkers will opt to pay more for an imported brand beer.

Egypt also produces its own **ouzo**. This is a strong, aniseed-flavoured clear spirit which turns milky when diluted. An even rougher aniseed-flavoured spirit called *zebib* is also available.

Egyptian **coffee** (*ahwa*) is similar to Greek or Turkish coffee and is served strong, sweet and in tiny cups. **Tea** (*shai*) usually comes by the glass, is served without milk and is also heavily sugared.

> **Juice Stalls**
> You will find fresh juice stalls all over Cairo and Luxor, catering to the local taste for freshly squeezed orange (*bortuaan*), guava (*guafa*), banana (*moz*), lemon (*limoon*), sugar cane (*asab*) and more – mix and match the flavours to invent your own juice cocktail.

Below: *For Egyptians, making tea for a guest is an elaborate ceremony.*

Where to Eat

Cairo has restaurants serving a number of different kinds of Egyptian, Middle Eastern and international cuisine, as well as dozens of **food stalls** selling delicious Egyptian snacks such as *taamiya* and kebabs.

Smaller Egyptian **restaurants** usually offer bean dishes such as *fuul*, a few meat dishes, roast or grilled chicken or pigeon, and possibly

Tea, coffee and tobacco

Islam frowns on alcohol, and for many Egyptians the stimulants of preference are, instead, tobacco, coffee and tea. In the Khan el-Khalili Bazaar (and in many other places) you can sit at a rickety café table to sample flavoured or plain tobacco in a nargileh, a tall water pipe which cools the tobacco smoke, though it still produces a distinct buzz. To go with it, order a glass of strong, sugary tea (*shai*) or mint tea (*shai naana*), or a thimble-sized cup of thick, muddy, Turkish-style coffee.

the tasty filled pancakes called *feteer*. They do not usually sell alcohol, but many serve fresh fruit juices along with bottled water or soft drinks.

The typical Egyptian **café** or *ahwa* usually has seats both indoors and spilling out onto the pavement, where local men sit with a coffee or a glass of tea, a nargileh (water pipe) of apple-flavoured tobacco, and a backgammon board. Less welcoming to visitors are local **bars** (sometimes called 'casinos', although they do not offer any gambling), which have an exclusively male clientele and are usually dimly lit and a little seedy. Better drinking establishments are to be found in all the larger hotels, and are popular with better-off Cairenes as well as hotel guests and visitors.

Mid-range tourist **hotels** in Cairo and Luxor offer fairly bland international cuisine, often (especially at breakfast and lunch) in the form of a buffet of salads, fruit, and imported cheeses and cold meats. Most luxury hotels have at least three restaurants, including a coffee shop, an international à la carte restaurant and an Egyptian/Middle Eastern restaurant.

Central Cairo

• LUXURY

Justine's

Named after the heroine of Lawrence Durrell's 'Alexandria Quartet' (which is set, despite its name, partly in Cairo), Justine's has a well-earned reputation for some of the best steaks in Cairo, and a fine *nouvelle cuisine* menu.

✉ *4 Sharia Hassan Sabri, El-Zamalek,*
☎ *(02) 736 2961.*

Citadel Grill

Of Cairo's dozens of luxury hotel restaurants, this is among the best, with a superb menu which focuses on grilled meat and seafood, classically cooked.

✉ *Ramses Hilton Hotel, 1115 Cornish el-Nil,* ☎ *(02) 575 4999.*

Naguib Mahfouz Café and Restaurant

Formerly the Khan el-Khalili Restaurant, this Cairo institution is now under the management of the

luxury Oberoi hotel group. No longer cheap, it nevertheless combines five-star menu and service with the timeless ambience of the Cairo bazaar area. The café serves Egyptian mint tea, Turkish-style coffee and fruit juices, and you can also sample one of their nargilehs. The restaurant has a fine menu of gourmet Egyptian dishes. Named after Egypt's most famous novelist, it is an experience not to be missed – even if your budget is small, it is worth a visit if only for one drink.

✉ *5 el-Badistan, Khan el-Khalili,*
☎ *(02) 590 3788.*

Above: *Smoking* shisha *and drinking tea in cafés are popular pastimes in Cairo.*
Opposite: *A vegetable market is the perfect to buy fresh produce while mingling with the locals.*

Baklava

Egyptians love the sweetest of dessert pastries, which come in all shapes and sizes. The desserts collectively known as baklava are made of phyllo pastry stuffed with nuts, honey or syrup and cut into various shapes. Similar stuffings and flavourings go into *kunafa*, made with bird's-nest-like strings of fried batter topping a creamy filling.

• MID-RANGE
Le Tabasco

The atmosphere is stylish, the menu is *nouvelle cuisine* with a French twist, and the prices at this friendly and casual restaurant are very affordable.

✉ *8 Midan Amman, Dokki,* ☎ *(02) 336 5583.*

Johnny Carino's

With indoor and outdoor seating on a moored boat and excellent service, this Italian restaurant is a good choice for lunch or dinner. The menu includes pizza, pasta dishes, grills, soups and salads. Serves beer but no wine.

✉ *between Kubri Qasr el-Nil and 6th of October bridges, El-Zamalek,* ☎ *(02) 735 3094.*

L'Aubergine

Pleasant vegetarian restaurant with an affordable and imaginative menu which blends Egyptian and Mediterranean influences in dishes such as moussaka, gnocchi, and spinach ravioli.

✉ *5 Sayed el-Bakry, El-Zamalek,* ☎ *(02) 738 0080.*

Five Bells

This superb garden restaurant is a great place for lunch, dinner or just an afternoon coffee. The menu blends Egyptian and European cuisine, the service is friendly and attentive, and the surroundings are pleasant, whether in the garden or in the prettily painted indoor restaurant. There is live jazz on Thursdays in the bar.

✉ *9 Sharia el-Adel Abou Bakr, El-Zamalek,* ☎ *(02) 735 8980.*

Arabesque Restaurant and Gallery

Handily located opposite the Egyptian Antiquities Museum, this restaurant serves Egyptian and European dishes in a dining room adorned with carved wooden screens and a shifting programme of works by contemporary Egyptian artists.

✉ *6 Qasr el-Nil,* ☎ *(02) 574 7898.*

• BUDGET
El Tekkia

One of a chain of modestly priced eating places, El Tekkia is an unpretentious spot and is a great place to sample typical Egyptian cooking, ranging from kofta, kebabs and bean salads to more daring dishes such as marinated liver and fried brain.

✉ *12 Midan Ibn Waleed, Dokki,* ☎ *(02) 749 6673.*

Papillon

This Lebanese restaurant in a mid-market shopping centre is a favourite with locals. The meze – up to a dozen mainly vegetarian dishes served simultaneously – is the best value choice.

✉ *Tersana Shopping Centre, Sharia 26 July, Mohandiseen,* ☎ *(02) 347 1600.*

Abu Tarek

This cheap, cheerful and (unusually for a budget joint) air-conditioned snack restaurant serves nourishing bowls of *kushari* – a thick mix of noodles, pulses, onions and tomato – at minimum prices.
⊠ *40 Sharia Champollion.*

The Coffee Roastery

Open until 02:00, the Coffee Roastery has three branches in central Cairo, all of them ideal spots to take the weight off your feet and enjoy a coffee, a soft drink, or one of their sandwiches or light meals.
Branches at ⊠ *11 road 18, Maadi,* ☎ *(02) 750 9914;* ⊠ *46 Nadi el-Said, Dokki,* ☎ *(02) 749 8882;* ⊠ *140 Sharia 26 July, El-Zamalek,* ☎ *(02) 738 0936.*

Grand Café

With a great location overlooking the Nile, the Grand Café serves grilled chicken, kofta, shish kebabs and *shawarma* and has an especially good range of fresh fruit salads and desserts. It stays open until well after midnight.
⊠ *Cornish el-Maadi,* ☎ *(02) 380 7017.*

Heliopolis

• *LUXURY*
La Casetta

Luxurious gourmet Italian restaurant serving good seafood dishes, imaginative pasta, grilled lamb, chicken and steak, and lavish desserts.
⊠ *32 Sharia Abd el Aziz Fahmi, Heliopolis,* ☎ *(02) 240 1555.*

• *MID-RANGE*
La Prima Vera

This Italian restaurant offers a very wide menu of pasta dishes, salads and desserts.
⊠ *42 Sharia Nabil el-Wakad, Heliopolis,* ☎ *(02) 415 5730.*

• *BUDGET*
Le Chantilly

A good spot for breakfast, lunch or dinner, Chantilly is a bakery, coffee shop and restaurant rolled into one, with a Western menu comprising snacks and pastries, fondue, pasta, pizza and salads, and seating indoors and outdoors.
⊠ *11 Sharia Baghdad,* ☎ *(02) 415 5620.*

Giza

• *LUXURY*
Seasons Restaurant

Finish off a day's sightseeing with dinner at one of Cairo's lushest restaurants, in the glamorous Four Seasons Hotel. The menu blends eastern and western Mediterranean influences, and the seafood buffet, though far from cheap, is superb.
⊠ *Four Seasons Hotel, 35 Sharia el-Giza, Giza,* ☎ *(02) 573 1212.*

• *MID-RANGE*
Americana Fish Market

Despite its name, the accent at this affordable Giza restaurant is

EATING OUT

on Egyptian-style seafood from the Mediterranean, moderately priced and open until the early hours of the morning.
⊠ *26 Sharia el-Nil, Giza,* ☎ *(02) 570 9693.*

The Orangerie

The 24-hour restaurant and coffee shop of the Movenpick Resort overlooks the hotel's lavish gardens and is handily close to the Pyramids.
⊠ *Movenpick Resort Cairo-Pyramids, Alexandria Road, Giza,* ☎ *(02) 385 2555.*

TGI Friday's

On the same moored boat as the Fish Market restaurant, TGI Friday's is part of the international restaurant chain and offers the usual array of burgers, steak, fries and lavish desserts. Westerners will find it comfortingly familiar: Egyptian diners, on the other hand, find it attractively exotic.
⊠ *26 Sharia el-Nil,* ☎ *(02) 570 9690.*

• *BUDGET*
Andrea's

This is an outdoor barbecue-chicken restaurant with a limited menu – grilled cuts of chicken or whole birds are served with Egyptian side dishes and dips. It is well worth a visit after a day at the pyramids.
⊠ *59 Sharia Marioutiyya,* ☎ *(02) 383 1133.*

Luxor (East Bank)
• *LUXURY*
The 1886

The gourmet restaurant of the Winter Palace Hotel is probably the most stylish, and certainly one of the more expensive places to eat in Luxor. Immaculate white-gloved waiters and candelabras set the tone, and men must wear jacket and tie. The menu is eclectic and international.
⊠ *Sofitel Winter Palace, Sharia Cornish el-Nil, Luxor,* ☎ *(095) 238 0422.*

Summer Night

Also located in the Winter Palace Hotel, the Summer Night restaurant in the gardens is delightful for dinner, and is one of the better places to sample the best of traditional Egyptian gourmet cooking.
⊠ *Sofitel Winter Palace, Sharia Cornish el-Nil, Luxor,* ☎ *(095) 238 0422.*

Le Lotus Boat

Luxury floating restaurant operated by the Novotel Luxor Hotel, offering five-star dining and sunset cruising on the Nile.
⊠ *Sharia Khalid Ibn el-Walid,* ☎ *(095) 238 0923.*

• *MID-RANGE*
King's Head Pub

Cold beer and soft drinks, coffee, juices, and snack meals are on offer at Luxor's favourite expat hangout, which also offers foreign and English-language Egyptian newspapers and magazines and a dartboard.

✉ Sharia Khalid Ibn el-Walid, ☎ (095) 237 1249.

• BUDGET
Jem's Restaurant

A good choice for vegetarians, with a meat-free set menu and a wider choice of Egyptian and international favourites, at prices to suit even the tightest budget.

✉ Sharia Khalid Ibn el-Walid, ☎ (095) 238 3604.

Luxor (West Bank)
• MID-RANGE
Al Gezira Rooftop Restaurant

Well-priced meals, cold Stella beers and a view of the Nile that is just as dramatic as those from the five-star hotels across the river – and at a much more affordable price. The cooking is mainly Egyptian, with a few international staples like grilled chicken.

✉ West Bank Ferry Landing, ☎ (095) 231 0034.

Tutankhamun Restaurant

Friendly, unassuming restaurant by the river serving an array of Egyptian vegetable and meat dishes, dips and salads, all at affordable prices.

✉ West Bank Ferry Landing, ☎ (095) 231 0118.

• BUDGET
Restaurant Mohammed

Very simple Egyptian restaurant serving chicken, duck, kebabs, and cold beer at cheap prices.

✉ next to Pharaohs Hotel, ☎ (095) 231 1014.

Eating Outside

Tempting as it is to eat alfresco in Cairo, it's not easy to find a suitable venue. Cairenes seem to ignore traffic fumes, noise and a constant stream of passers-by, not to mention scorching summer heat and chilly winter evenings. Westerners may prefer the slightly calmer environs of El-Zamalek to the frenetic surroundings of the city centre, and to escape from the pressures of the city streets the best bet can be the poolside restaurant of one of the big hotels.

Below: Luxor is surrounded by farming villages, and villagers like this fruit vendor bring their fresh produce to sell in the daily market.

ENTERTAINMENT
Nightlife

Cairo buzzes after dark, especially in summer, when people come out to shop and socialize in the cool of the evening. Serious nightlife does not begin until later – from around 22:00 – and continues until at least 03:00, with some of the livelier casinos staying open until dawn. There is plenty of choice, ranging from low-life 'baladi' bars favoured by an exclusively male, working-class Egyptian clientele to Western-style music bars with live musicians or DJs, cosmopolitan nightclubs and discos.

More tolerant of a range of peccadilloes than many of its neighbours, Cairo has a vibrant nightlife – a magnet for well-off patrons of everything from belly dancing to casino gambling, from all over the Middle East. There are regular **belly-dancing** shows in most of the major hotels and at several nightclubs and restaurants in the Giza area. These are patronized mainly by European and Middle Eastern tourists. For many Cairo dwellers, Thursdays and

What's On?

Check the monthly, English-language magazine *Egypt Today* (or its website, 🖳 www.egypttoday.com) for news and reviews of the latest events and nightspots. You'll also find events listings in the English-language edition of the weekly *Al-Ahram* and in the *Egyptian Gazette*. Whereas Cairo is one of the world's largest capital cities, Luxor is really a small town. There is no real night-life scene, though the major hotels all have rather lacklustre disco-clubs. Not to be missed is the nightly, multi-lingual Sound and Light presentation at the Temple of Karnak, one of Egypt's more memorable experiences.

Fridays are the nights for going out, with Friday and Saturday being days off for most people and Sunday a working day. Many Egyptians eschew alcohol and stick to coffee and soft drinks all night, but alcoholic drinks are readily available in all up-scale nightlife venues.

Music

Cairo's somewhat limited live music scene ranges from a handful of jazz bars and music cafés with performances by local and visiting musicians, middle-of-the-road rock and pop live – and on disc at hotel discos and independent clubs – and Arabic and Western classical music at two main venues. The **Cairo Opera House** hosts performances of opera, ballet and classical music by visiting ensembles and the Cairo Symphony Orchestra. Its vast auditorium seats 1200 and has excellent acoustics. There is a smaller hall, seating 500, and an outdoor theatre. There are also occasional performances of classical Arabic music. The **Arabic Music Institute** is Cairo's main venue for classical Arabic music, song and dance and is the home of the Umm Kalthoum Classical Arabic Music Troupe, named after the Egyptian traditional music world's most famous singer.

Theatre

Cairo has a number of popular theatres, but their productions are exclusively in Arabic and are closer in spirit to Western vaudeville or variety – a barrage of puns, broad humour, song and dance, all in Arabic – which may well amuse local audiences but generally leave the visitor cold.

Cairo Opera House
✉ Gezira Exhibition Grounds, Gezira Island
☎ (02) 739 8144
🖥 www.cairooperahouse.org
M Opera
🕐 open for performances only; box office open 09:00–12:00 and 14:00–18:00

Arabic Music Institute
✉ 22 Sharia Ramses, Downtown
☎ (02) 574 3373

Opposite: *The Sound and Light Show at Giza is a must for night-time entertainment.*
Below: *Garish larger-than-life murals advertise locally produced movies.*

Casino d'Egypt
✉ Mena House Oberoi
Hotel, Pyramids Road,
Giza
☎ (02) 383 3222
🕐 10:00–05:00

Casino Ramses Hilton
✉ Ramses Hilton Hotel,
1115 Cornish el-Nil
☎ (02) 574 4400
🖳 www.hilton.com
🕐 15:00–09:00

Movenpick Casino
✉ Movenpick
Heliopolis Hotel, PO
Box 2741, El-Horreya,
Heliopolis
☎ (02) 637 0077
📧 email@
movenpick.com.eg
🕐 17:30–09.00

**Omar Khayyam
Casino**
✉ Cairo Marriott
Hotel, Sharia el-Gezira,
El-Zamalek
☎ (02) 735 8888
📧 marriott@
ritsec3.com.eg
🕐 24 hours

Casinos

Casino gambling is one of the major attractions for many visitors to Cairo, and the city has more than a dozen up-scale gaming establishments, most of which are attached to the five-star hotels. (For details of Cairo's casinos, see panel on this page.)

Casinos are open only to non-Egyptians, and you will have to show your passport to gain access. Games on offer at the casinos include roulette, blackjack, poker, punto blanco and the inevitable slot machines and video games.

Festivals

One of the biggest and most important celebrations in the Islamic calendar is **Eid el-Fitr**, when the end of the fasting month of **Ramadan** is marked by three days of feasting and present-giving. This festival is mainly a family affair.

A livelier and more public festival is *Moulid el-Nabi* (12th day of Rabei el-Awal), which is marked by processions in Cairo, Luxor and nationwide.

Spectator Sports

Cairo's most popular spectator sport is **football**. The city has two main teams, Zamalek and Al-Ahly, which are fierce rivals although they share the city's **Cairo Stadium**, out at Heliopolis, where matches are played every weekend from September through to May.

Not far from the Cairo Stadium is the **Heliopolis Hippodrome**, where you can watch **horse racing** from October to May, and there is also racing in winter at **El-Gezira Sporting Club** on Gezira Island.

Rowing on the Nile (a legacy of the British occupation) is also popular with better-off Cairenes and expats, with teams from several Cairo clubs competing most Fridays, usually starting from the East Bank near Giza. Races are co-ordinated by **Al-Nil Sporting Club**.

In addition, Cairo hosts some major annual **sporting events**, including the Egypt International Tennis Championship in February; the Pharaohs' Rally, at Giza, each October, and the Arabian Horse Festival in November. In Luxor, an International Marathon is run along the banks of the Nile in February.

Comprehensive listings of several upcoming sporting events can be found in the *Egyptian Gazette*.

Birqash Camel Market

It's not uncommon to see camels laden with goods being driven through the streets of Cairo and Luxor, and they are even more common in the countryside. The Birqash Camel Market, 35km (21 miles) northwest of the city centre, is the largest of its kind in Egypt. A visit here is memorable, not least for the noise and smell of hundreds of these ungainly, half-wild beasts.

Egyptian Literature
Cairo-born **Naguib Mahfouz** (1911–2006) is the colossus of Egyptian literature. He won the Nobel Prize for Literature in 1988 and is best known for the *Cairo Trilogy*, which narrates the story of a Cairo family through several generations. A number of other Egyptian authors are widely published in foreign languages, including Alaa Al Aswany, whose novel *The Yacoubian Building* (a lively look at sex, corruption, and extremism in modern Egypt) has become a bestseller in 17 languages.

Sports Venues
Zamalek Football Club
☎ (02) 417 0010
Al-Ahly FC
☎ (02) 735 2114
Heliopolis Hippodrome
☎ (02) 241 7086/7134
El-Gezira Sporting Club ☎ (02) 736 0434
Al-Nil Sporting Club
☎ (02) 393 4350)

Opposite: *Moulids are the most colourful events in the Nile Delta.*

Above: *Famous Fifi Abdou, one of Cairo's hottest (and most highly paid) belly dancers, performs in a five-star nightclub.*

Nightclubs, Bars and Discos

Hard Rock Café

One of Cairo's newer nightspots, part of the international Hard Rock chain, is decorated with rock-and-roll memorabilia and turns into a dance venue with live music after midnight.
✉ *Grand Hyatt, Roda Island,*
☎ *(02) 532 1277.*

Jackie's Joint

This is Cairo's longest established disco, with a bafflingly strict door policy which makes it difficult to get in unless you are a hotel guest. It offers rather bland music and very expensive drinks, but is still one of Cairo's most popular nightspots.
✉ *Nile Hilton Hotel,*
☎ *(02) 578 0444.*

Nile Pharaoh Floating Restaurant

Belly dancers, giddily spinning dervishes, singers and musicians make this three-hour dinner cruise on the Nile an experience to remember.
✉ *31 Sharia el-Nil,*
☎ *(02) 570 1000.*

NIGHTCLUBS, BARS & DISCOS

Taverne du Champs de Mars

This is the longest established and most popular of Cairo's posh hotel bars, patronized by wealthy Cairenes and expats as well as hotel guests and visitors.
✉ Nile Hilton Hotel, Midan el-Tahrir,
☎ (02) 578 0444.

Harry's Pub

Fake British-style pub with darts, sports on TV, beer in tankards and cheesy lounge acts. Great fun, despite all that.
✉ Cairo Marriott Hotel, El-Zamalek,
☎ (02) 735 8888.

Black Cat Café

This relaxed café-bar upstairs from l'Aubergine restaurant offers live jazz on Thursdays and Fridays, and the occasional jam session featuring local and visiting musicians (see also l'Aubergine, page 68).
✉ 5 Sayed al Bakry, El-Zamalek, ☎ (02) 738 0080.

After 8

Popular restaurant/bar with live music at weekends, when you will need to book
✉ 6 Qasr el Nil, Downtown,
☎ (02) 574 0855.

Odeon Bar

On the top floor of the Odeon Hotel. Eat, drink, and smoke shisha 24-hours a day while looking out over the roofs of downtown Cairo.
✉ 6 Sharia Abd el Hamid, off Talaat Harb, Downtown,
☎ (02) 576 7971.

Estoril

Old-style restaurant and bar from the 1950s with good food and great atmosphere.
✉ 12 Sharia Talaat Harb, Downtown,
☎ (02) 574 3102.

Cairo Jazz Club

Live music, cold drinks and dim lighting are features of the city's leading live jazz venue, in Mohandiseen.
✉ 197 Sharia 26 July,
☎ (02) 345 9939.

Bes and Taweret

Fat and gnome-like Bes was the Egyptian god of **music and dancing** and also one of the protectors of both pregnant women and newborn babies, whom he guarded against the demons. Taweret, with the head of a hippo, the legs of a lioness and the tail of a crocodile, also protected women in childbirth.

Omm Kolthum

The voice you hear singing plaintive Egyptian songs over your hotel sound system, on the radio, or on the cassette deck of your coach or taxi is as likely as not to be that of **Omm Kolthum**. Though she died in 1975, the Egyptian singer shaped modern Arab music not just in Egypt but across the Arab world. She came on the scene at a time when Egypt was being reshaped, and is still very much perceived as one of the voices of the Egyptian people.

EXCURSIONS

You can easily combine Egypt and Luxor in one holiday, spending three to four days in each place and travelling between them by air or – more adventurously – by overnight sleeper train. But Egypt offers an array of other destinations which can be combined with Cairo, Luxor, or both.

Alexandria, Egypt's second city, is 225km (130 miles) northwest of Cairo, a 2-hour train ride or 3-hour road journey through the Nile Delta. Its attractions include the 15th-century Citadel, several museums, and the new $200 million Library of Alexandria.

For a spell on the beach, the most accessible resort is **Sharm el-Sheikh**, on the tip of the Sinai Peninsula, which has superb water sports, world-class scuba diving and plenty of mid-range and luxury accommodation.

The **river journey** between Luxor and Aswan, the southernmost navigable point on the Nile, can be a most romantic experience, whether you charter an open felucca with crew, or travel in luxury on one of the many 'floating hotel' cruise ships operated by several of Egypt's leading five-star hotels. These cruises offer you fascinating glimpses of life on and beside the Nile, as well as visiting riverside temple sites such as Edfu, Esna and Kom Ombo.

Still further south from Luxor, the stupendous cliffside colossi and temples at **Abu Simbel** can be visited in one day by air, or combined with a trip to Aswan.

Another popular option is combining a visit to Luxor with a few days on the Red Sea at **Hurghada**, a purpose-built resort town which offers a wide range of water sports and good scuba diving.

The Great Library

The Arab conquerors of the 7th century AD are often blamed for the sack of Alexandria's Great Library, at one time the greatest storehouse of knowledge in the world. Alexandria was sacked and burned by the Arabs in 646, but by then most of the library's manuscripts had already been destroyed – by Christian bishops who anathematized their secular learning and their pagan philosophy, or by monks who recycled the precious parchments and used them to write Christian texts.

Alexandria

This bustling city of more than four million people is Egypt's second largest, and is very different from Cairo. The city lies in a long strip along the Mediterranean coast, and inland, beyond the suburbs, are the lakes, river channels and green fields of the Nile Delta. A major Mediterranean seaport since ancient times (it was founded in the 4th century BC by Alexander the Great), it was, until Egypt's nationalist revolution in the 1950s, a cosmopolitan city, with a large Greek population, most of whom have now emigrated. It was one of the most important cities of the Roman Empire, and Roman remains include a 3rd century AD **Roman Amphitheatre** (Kom el Dik), **Roman Baths**, and a **stone column** erected to mark the victories of the 3rd-century Emperor Diocletian, erroneously known as 'Pompey's Pillar', a name given to it by ill-informed medieval crusaders.

Remnants of the Mameluke era include **Qaytbay's Fortress**, a 15th-century castle whose round towers dominate the harbour. It now houses the city's **Naval Museum**, while a fine **Graeco-Roman Museum** houses a collection of finds dating back to the Ptolemaic era, including a superb granite sculpture of the Bull of Apis and busts of both Mark Anthony and Cleopatra. Other sights in Alexandria include 2nd-century BC catacombs as well as rock tombs.

> **Alexandria**
> **Location:** Maps D, J–C1
> **Distance from Cairo:** 225 km (130 miles) northwest of Cairo
> ⊕ 09:00–16:00 daily, closed 11:30–13:30 on Fridays (Naval Museum)
> ⊕ 09:00–16:00 daily, closed 11:30–13:30 on Fridays (Roman Amphitheatre)
> ⊕ 09:00–16:00 daily, closed 11:30–13:30 on Fridays (Graeco-Roman Museum)

Opposite: *The stone column of Diocletian is often wrongly called Pompey's Pillar.*
Below: *This Roman amphitheatre could seat 800 spectators.*

Limerick
County Library

Sharm el-Sheikh
Location: Map J–F3
Distance from Cairo:
500km (310 miles)
southeast of Cairo

Sharm el-Sheikh
Tourist Office
✉ Port Authority
Building
☎ (062) 360 0170

Opposite: *For those with a sense of adventure, nothing beats a felucca cruise on the Nile.*
Below: *Aerial view of Râs Muhammed, the finest marine conservation area of the Red Sea.*

Sharm el-Sheikh

On a promontory where the Gulf of Aqaba opens into the Red Sea, Sharm el-Sheikh was a tiny trading port and fishing harbour on the edge of the empty Sinai Desert until the Israeli occupation of the Sinai in 1967, after which it became a small holiday resort for Israeli visitors. After being handed back to Egypt in 1982, Sharm became a popular destination for scuba divers because of its fine coral reefs close inshore, some of which are now protected by the **Râs Muhammed National Park**. Visibility is usually excellent and, although the coral reef has suffered from damage and global warming, there's still plenty of marine life to see, including rays, sharks, lion fish and morays. Popular dive sites outside the park include the **wrecks** of the *Dunraven*, sunk in 1876, the *Carnatic*, which went down in 1879, and the *Thistlegorm*, sunk by bombing during World War II.

Sharm el-Sheikh has now grown into a full-scale holiday resort, catering not just to scuba divers but also to European visitors in search of guaranteed winter sunshine. It has merged with **Na'ama Bay**, some 6km (3.5 miles) to the east, forming a continuous strip of restaurants and hotels, from mid-range properties to excellent all-inclusive luxury resorts.

Nile Cruise from Luxor to Aswan

A leisurely cruise on one of the dozens of purpose-built 'floating hotels' which ply the upper reaches of the Nile between Luxor and Aswan is a delightfully relaxed way to see life on the Nile, and a string of remarkable ancient temples on the banks of the river. Most of the major hotel chains with properties in Cairo or Luxor operate their own luxury cruisers, with elegant dining, roomy cabins and on-board pools and sundecks. There are also cheaper, smaller cruisers operated by independent tour and travel agencies. State-owned **Misr Travel** (*see page 49*) has its own river flotilla.

Most river cruisers carry their own complement of guides and guest lecturers, and call at important temple sites along the Upper Nile including the temple of the ram-headed god **Khnum** at Esna, the **Temple of Horus** at Edfu, with its colossal gateway guarded by giant stone falcons, and the **Temple of Sobek and Haroeris** at Kom Ombo. At Aswan, there are ruins worth seeing on **Elephantine Island**, on the Nile, and **Philae**, an island in Lake Nasser. There is also an interesting small museum.

You can make the Nile journey either way, spending two to four nights on board and returning to Cairo by air from Aswan or to Luxor by coach or air. You can also travel more cheaply and adventurously – and in a lot less luxury – by hiring an open felucca with skipper and crew from the waterfront at Aswan, where strenuous bargaining will be called for.

Temple of Khnum, Esna
Location: Map J–E4
Distance from Luxor: 60km (38 miles) south of Luxor
🕐 06:00–17:30 winter, 06:00–18.30 summer

Temple of Horus, Edfu
Location: Map J–E5
Distance from Luxor: 115 km (70 miles) south of Luxor
🕐 07:00–16:00 winter, 06:00–18:00 summer

Temple of Sobek and Haroeris, Kom Ombo
Location: Map J–E5
Distance from Aswan: 40km (25 miles) north of Aswan
🕐 08:00–16:00

Nubia Museum
✉ Behind the Cataract Hotel, Aswan
🕐 09:00–13:00, 17:00–20:00

Above: *The colossal statues at Abu Simbel were relocated to save them from the rising waters of Lake Nasser.*

Abu Simbel

The awe-inspiring temples and colossal statues that stand close to the banks of Lake Nasser at Abu Simbel are a tribute to modern engineering skills as well as to their ancient builders. As the waters rose behind the High Dam at Aswan, threatening to inundate the enormous effigies of **Ramses II**, the huge statues were carefully dismantled, then removed from their original site and meticulously rebuilt against an artificial cliff some 65m (213ft) above the waterline. The project was completed in 1968.

Four gigantic, seated figures of the pharaoh – each some 20m (65ft) tall and standing on a 4m (13ft) plinth – are on guard at the entrance to the **Great Temple of Ramses II**, and a statue of the hawk-headed sun god Ra stands above the entrance. Inside, the temple is a riot of carvings showing Ramses II defeating the Hittites at the battle of Kadesh, and statues of Ra, Ramses II, Amun and Ptah sit in the inner sanctum.

Next to the Great Temple of Ramses II is the much smaller – but still very striking – **Temple of Hathor**, the cow-headed goddess. It is fronted by six 10m (33ft) colossi of Ramses II, his queen, Nefertari, and their sons and daughters.

__Abu Simbel__
Location: Map J–D6
Distance from
Aswan: 300km (180 miles) south of Aswan (You can take a flight from Cairo, Luxor or Aswan)
🕑 07:00–16:00 winter, 07:00–17:00 summer

ABU SIMBEL & HURGHADA

Hurghada

Hurghada, on the west shore of the Red Sea, is a somewhat chaotic strip of tourism development stretching for about 30–40km (20–30 miles) to the north and south of the original fishing harbour and seaport town of **Ghardaqa** which is making an uneasy transition into a full-scale resort complete with international bars, restaurants and nightclubs. Its beaches are nothing to get excited about, made as they are of a gritty red sand, but there are plenty of excellent holiday hotels at bargain prices – hardly surprising, considering that it has some 90,000 hotel beds competing to be filled. The resort is popular with package holiday-makers from northern Europe – including Russians, Ukrainians and Scandinavians as well as Britons – in winter, with regular international charter flights. It also has some good scuba diving, around the inshore **Giftûn Islands**, and is a popular place to learn to dive. Underwater fauna include white-tipped sharks, eagle rays and giant morays, and efforts are being made to protect the coral reefs and their marine denizens.

About 62km (38 miles) to the north of Hurghada's airport is the purpose-built resort of **El-Gouna**. It is a little more luxurious and also somewhat better planned than the Hurghada strip.

Hurghada
Location: Map J–E3
Distance from Luxor: 270km (167 miles) northeast of Luxor (There are flights and buses from Luxor, and flights from Cairo)

Below: *Heading out by boat to the superb dive sites off Hurghada.*

Above: *Traffic chaos in Cairo is an everyday occurrence.*

Package Tours
Even if you are a free spirit, taking a package holiday (including flights, transfers, accommodation and guided tours) from your home country can be the most affordable way of seeing Egypt. It eliminates the constant hassle of finding your way around and bargaining over everything from hotel rooms and taxis to camel and felucca hire. For details of tour operators specializing in trips to Egypt, *see* pages 45–49.

Best Times to Visit

Cairo and Luxor are best visited between October and May, when daytime temperatures average between 25°C and 30°C. It almost never rains in Luxor, and rain is rare in Cairo, with an average monthly rainfall of less than 5mm (0.22in) between October and May. Nights can be cool in Luxor and chilly in Cairo at this time of year. Avoid visiting between late May and late September, when temperatures reach as high as 40°C and Cairo suffers unpleasant air pollution.

Tourist Information

The **Egyptian Tourist Authority** has offices in London, New York, San Francisco, Chicago, Johannesburg and Montreal. There are local tourist information offices in **Cairo** at ⌧ 5 Sharia Adly, ☎ (02) 391 3454; ⌧ Pyramid Rd, ☎ (02) 383 8823; ⌧ Ramses Railway Station, ☎ (02) 579 0767; and ⌧ Cairo International Airport, ☎ (02) 291 4255; and at **Luxor** at ⌧ Sharia el-Nil (next to the Luxor Museum), ☎ (095) 237 2009. The official website of the Egyptian Tourist Authority has comprehensive listings of attractions, museums, monuments, activities, hotels and restaurants; visit 🖥 www.interoz.com/egypt Other useful websites include www.cairotourist.com (the official Cairo tourism website); www.egypttoday.com (the very useful and entertaining online edition of *Egypt Today* magazine, with news, cultural information, and hotel and restaurant reviews); www.egyptianmuseum.com (the official site of the Egyptian Antiquities Museum); www.copticmuseum.gov.eg (the official site of the Coptic Museum); and www.cim.gov.eg (the official site of the Cairo Islamic Monuments).

Entry Requirements

All visitors require a national passport with at least six months' validity. All foreign visitors require visas, obtainable on arrival or in advance from your nearest Egyptian consulate. Note that visas are valid for a month only, and you will not be allowed to leave Egypt with an out-of-date visa.

Customs

Duty-free allowances are as follows:
1 litre (1 quart) spirits, 1 litre (1 quart) perfume, 200 cigarettes and 25 cigars. Duty-free goods are available on arrival at international airports. Travellers with video cameras or laptop computers may be required to fill in a form on arrival, guaranteeing that they will re-export them on departure.

Health Requirements

Proof of immunization against cholera and yellow fever is required for those arriving from infected areas, including southern Africa and South America. No other immunizations are mandatory.

Getting There

By air: Cairo International Airport is around 25km (15 miles) northeast of the centre (about 30–60 minutes by taxi, depending on traffic).

For flight information, ☎ (02) 634 8566, . www.cairo-airport.com There are direct flights to Cairo from all of the European capitals and other major cities in Europe, and also from the USA, Canada, Australia, most African states, and all Middle Eastern capitals.
Luxor International Airport is around 16km (10 miles) from the city centre (20–30 minutes by taxi). For flight information, ☎ (095) 237 2306. There are a few direct flights to Luxor from European cities, as well as seasonal (winter) charter flights direct to Luxor from some British and mainland European cities which are sold as part of a package holiday including accommodation.
By road: Express coach services connect Cairo with Luxor and via Suez and Sinai with Eilat in Israel. Car rental is available from a range of international agencies with offices at Cairo and Luxor air-

ports and in downtown Cairo, but self-drive hire is neither necessary nor recommended. Roads are poor, many Egyptian vehicles are poorly maintained, and road safety standards are very low.

If you do rent, use a reputable international chain. An international driving licence is required. Carry your licence and all vehicle papers at all times as they must be produced at police checkpoints. Take out the maximum insurance, including collision damage waiver, as the risk of an accident is high. Drive defensively as other vehicles are usually driven recklessly and at high speed. The official speed limit is 90kph (55mph) on ordinary highways and 100kph (64mph) on four-lane motorways, but this limit is generally ignored. Do not drive at night unless absolutely necessary. Drive on the right, but be aware that off main highways (and often even on them) signposting hardly exists and is usually in Arabic.

By bus: Long-distance buses operate between Cairo and Luxor. Fares are cheap, and express buses are sometimes faster than trains. You cannot book tickets or obtain timetable information by telephone; if you are in a cheap hotel frequented by budget travellers, you may be able to buy tickets at the hotel. Otherwise arrange transport in person at the bus station. Tight security against terrorism means that plainclothes policemen ride shotgun on many inter-city buses. On some of the routes, tourists are required to travel on special services in convoy.

Shared Taxis: Between towns and villages, many Egyptians travel by shared taxis which travel a set route and depart when full – very full. Taxi travel is hair-raising, but in some areas it may be the only option. Shared taxis usually congregate at stands close to main local bus or rail stations.

By rail: There are no international rail services. Two express trains daily, and an overnight sleeper service, connect Cairo and Luxor. First class is comfortable, second class reasonable, third class only for the desperate. Reservations and information are not available by telephone, and often impossible even in person. Book rail tickets through your hotel or local travel agency, at least three days in advance.

Cairo: ✉ Ramses Station, Midan Ramses, 🕐 24 hours. First, second- and third-class trains to all destinations; Wagons-Lits sleeping cars to Luxor and Aswan. For berths, ☎ and 📠 (02) 795 2966, or go to 🖥 www.sleepingtrains.com

Luxor: ✉ Luxor

Station, Midan el-Mahatta, ⏱ 24 hours. For information, ☎ (095) 237 0259.

What to Pack

Egypt is a conservative Muslim society. Shorts, T-shirts and beachwear are acceptable only in resorts on the Red Sea which receive many European tourists, and even then only on the beach. Revealing garments are frowned on and encourage unwelcome attention. Light long-sleeved shirts or blouses, long trousers and frocks will not offend local sensibilities and are also a sensible precaution against the sun. Women may be required to wear a headscarf in religious buildings. In winter, nights can be chilly even in Upper Egypt. Pack a medium-weight sweater or jacket. Mosquito repellent containing 'deet' (diethyltoluamide) is the best. Photographers using slide or specialist film

should take a plentiful supply as only standard film is usually available locally. Sunglasses protect eyes against fierce sun, dust and urban air pollution.

Money Matters

The Egyptian pound is divided into 100 piastres. Egyptian currency is not always obtainable abroad. US dollars, sterling and euros are readily exchangeable at banks and hotels. Small-denomination notes and coins can be very useful in view of demands for baksheesh (tips) from guides, porters, boatmen, taxi and carriage drivers, gatekeepers and beggars. The best way to carry money is in travellers' cheques in smaller denominations (e.g. UK£20 or US$50) to avoid carrying a lot of cash at any time. Banks normally offer a better rate of exchange, or charge less commission, than hotel desks or money-changers. Do not be tempted by offers to

Camels

The camel may well be a quite recent arrival to Egypt. Ubiquitous now (especially around main tourist attractions) the dromedary is conspicuously absent from ancient paintings and inscriptions, and may not have arrived in numbers until the Arab conquest. Several tour operators offer desert safaris by camel, but be warned: it is one of the least comfortable mounts in the world.

Safety and Security

Since the attack on tourists at the Temple of Hatshepsut in Luxor in November 1997, armed plain-clothes policemen accompany all organized tour groups at ancient sites in Luxor, Cairo and elsewhere, and armed uniformed police guard most large hotels, visitor attractions and public buildings. Tourist coaches between Cairo and Luxor and between Luxor and Hurghada on the Red Sea travel in guarded convoys.

Important Notice

At the time of going to press, Greater Cairo telephone numbers were being upgraded to 8 digits. On numbers in Cairo Governorate, add a 2 at the beginning; on Giza numbers add 3; and on Qalyubiya numbers add 4.

exchange money on the black market which in practice no longer exists; such offers are scams. Credit cards are accepted in larger hotels, restaurants and shops in Cairo and the main tourist areas, but not really elsewhere. ATMs accepting Visa, Master and Cirrus cards are now widely available.

Transport

Cairo's modern, air-conditioned **metro** network is a welcome contrast to the chaos above ground. There are two lines, one running between El-Marg in the northeast and Helwan in the south, the other between Giza and Shubra el-Kheima. The lines intersect in the city centre at Sadat (Midan el-Tahrir) and Mubarak (Midan Ramses) stations. Fares are extremely cheap and trains run from 05:00–23:30. Metro stations are indicated by a large red M with-

in a five-pointed blue star.

Black-and-white taxis are cheap but the meter is never used and fares are always a matter for negotiation: aim to pay no more than half the first asking price. Recommended fares to all destinations are displayed at airport terminals and many of the hotels. The new **yellow cabs** offer a more comfortable ride at metered rates but are not yet widespread. Sightseeing tour coaches are probably the best way of getting to Giza, Saqqara or Memphis, as long as you do not mind being in a group.

Open-topped **horse-drawn carriages** (calèches or *hantours*) ply the corniches of both Luxor and Cairo. Negotiate a price before boarding. Many **river cruisers** or 'floating hotels' operate on the Nile. There are currently no cruises between Cairo and Luxor but cruises do operate between Luxor and Aswan in each direction and are included in the brochures of most international tour operators to Egypt.

Business Hours

Government offices: ⏰ 09:00–14:00, most closed Fridays and Saturdays. Banks and commercial offices: ⏰ 08:30–13:30, most are closed on Fridays and Saturdays.

Time Difference

GMT +2 in winter, GMT +3 in summer.

Communications

The international dialling code for Egypt is (+20). The code for Cairo is (02) and the code for Luxor is (095). Omit the (0) when calling internationally. Telephones are available in most hotels, and metered telephones in cafés and restaurants. There is normally a substantial minimum charge for international calls from hotels, and prices may be heavily loaded. In Cairo you can also make international calls from the PTT offices at ✉ Midan el-Tahrir, Sharia Alfi Bey and Sharia Adly, ⏰ all open 24 hours. Fax services are also available from hotels and at PTT offices. Street payphones have recently become widespread. GSM mobile phone coverage in Cairo and Luxor is adequate.

The international dialling codes from Egypt are: UK (00 44); Australia (00 61); New Zealand (00 64); USA and Canada (00 1); South Africa (00 67); Ireland (00 353). Enquiries ☎ 140. The Cairo Central Post Office at ✉ Midan el-Ataba is open ⏰ 24 hours. Other post offices ⏰ open 08:30–15:00, closed Friday. It is much easier to post letters and postcards from your hotel, which will sell stamps. Letters weighing less than 100g (4oz) can be sent by premium rate Express Mail.

Electricity

The power system used in Egypt is 220V AC. Sockets take European-style two-pin plugs. Visitors from North America using appliances running on 110V AC will beed a transformer. British visitors will need a plug adapter.

Weights and Measures

The metric system is used in Egypt.

Health Precautions

Seek medical advice regarding immunizations, including those against meningitis, hepatitis, polio, tetanus, typhoid and diphtheria. Tap water should not be trusted, even in Cairo. Bottled water is available. Bilharzia, an infestation carried by water snails, is prevalent in Egypt and can damage internal organs. Do not swim in the Nile at any point, and consider seeking medical treatment if you do happen to fall in. Use a high-factor sun block when sailing, sunbathing, or even walking around town. Wear a hat at archeological sites, where there is little shade. Especially in summer, be sure to drink plenty of water – you may not feel yourself sweating, but the dry air dehydrates your body very quickly.

Health Services

Public health services are limited and good private hospitals are only found in Cairo. Make sure you have adequate insurance to cover the cost of private health care in case of accident or illness, including medical repatriation expenses.

Personal Safety

Between 1992 and 1997 extremists conducted a campaign of violence against the government, and there have been a few further attacks since then.

The last was in 2005 when 88 people were killed in coordinated suicide bombings in Sharm el Sheikh. Security has been heightened since the 1990s, but visitors are advised to be vigilant and respect advice from security authorities. Terrorism aside, violent crime against visitors is rare, though theft and pickpocketing are rife. Watch your belongings at all times, use hotel safes if available, and keep travellers' cheques, money and tickets on your person in a concealed wallet, inner pocket or moneybelt. Be especially wary on city buses. Road accidents are frequent and windscreens may be smashed by flying pebbles. Avoid sitting in the front seat of taxis or minibuses and do not travel in these at night.

Have absolutely nothing to do with drugs. The minimum sentence for bringing drugs into Egypt is 25 years in prison, and even the death sentence could be applicable in the case of a drugs offence.

Emergencies

Cairo emergencies: **Ambulance ☎ 123; Fire brigade ☎ 125; Police ☎ 122; Tourist Police ☎ 126.** Do not count on any of these speaking English.

Etiquette

Wearing skimpy clothes away from Red Sea resorts will offend Egyptian sensibilities (see What to Pack). Remove shoes when entering a place of worship or a private home. Women may be asked to cover their heads inside a mosque or church. Egypt has a relaxed attitude to alcohol, but public drunkenness is strongly disapproved of. Public displays of affection between the sexes are taboo, though Egyptian men embrace on meeting and are often seen holding hands.

Do not photograph people without their permission, and do not take photographs of or near military installations.

Language

Arabic, in its Egyptian dialect, is the national language, but English is spoken in hotels and by shopkeepers and guides.

Holidays and Festivals

The Islamic calendar differs from the Western, with 12 lunar months and a year that is 11 days shorter, so holidays arrive 10–12 days earlier each year. As they depend on the first sighting of the new moon, dates cannot accurately be predicted far in advance. Major events of the Egyptian year include:

Ramadan – the month of fasting, during which Muslims may not eat between sunrise and sunset; they tend to make up for this after dark.

Most government offices have shorter working hours during Ramadan.

Eid el-Fitr – three-day celebration of the end of Ramadan, mainly a family festival, with new clothes for all and much eating. Avoid travel during Eid, when all Egypt is on the move.

Moulid el-Nabi (the 12th day of Rabei el-Awal) – feast of the Prophet's Birthday, with processions in Cairo and elsewhere.

Eid el-Adha (10th day of Zoul Higga) – culmination of pilgrimage (hadj) to Mecca. Public transport is crowded by pilgrims.

Sham el-Nessim (mid-April) – follows Coptic Easter (on different dates each year) and is a national holiday. Apart from religious festivals, Egypt also has **public holidays** on 25 April (Sinai Liberation Day); 1 May (May Day); 23 July (Revolution Day); and 6 October (National Day).

Useful Phrases

Inshallah • God willing (used in sentences such as: the coach will leave at one o'clock, *inshallah*

Maalesh • never mind

Bukra • tomorrow (or the day after)

Shwayya shwayya • slow down, take it easy

Min fadlak (**M**), *min fadlik* (**F**) • please

Shokran • thank you

Lah, shokran • no, thank you

Aywa • yes

Lah • no

INDEX OF SIGHTS

GENERAL INDEX

GENERAL INDEX